WE THE GEN Z

What the Constitution Actually Says and Why You Should Care

No boring legal jargon! Your rights, your voice!

MALLORY DAIN

WE THE GEN Z
What the Constitution Actually Says and Why You Should Care

Copyright © 2025 by Mallory Dain
First edition, February 2025. Published by Studio Graphio.
ISBN: 979-8-9916737-9-2
Cover and interior design by Mallory Dain.
Digital typeface: Mr. Eaves

All rights reserved. No part of this book may be reproduced or transmitted in any form or by any means—electronic, mechanical, photocopy, recording, or otherwise—without prior written permission from the publisher, except for brief quotes used in reviews or educational materials.

While every effort has been made to ensure the accuracy of the information in this book, the authors assume no responsibility for errors or omissions. The content is for educational and informational purposes only and does not constitute legal advice.

Table of Contents

Introduction 7

The Constitution of the United States of America ... 17
    The Preamble 18
    Article I: The Legislative Branch 21
    Article II: The Executive Branch 65
    Article III: The Judicial Branch 83
    Article IV: How States Work Together 91
    Article V: How to Change the Constitution 97
    Article VI: The Constitution is the Supreme Law 101
    Article VII: How the Constitution Was Approved 105

The Bill of Rights 109
    Amendment I: Your Basic Freedoms 115
    Amendment II: The Right to Keep and Bear Arms 122
    Amendment III: Ban on Forced Housing of Troops 125
    Amendment IV: Protection from Unreasonable
        Searches and Seizures 127
    Amendment V: The Right to Due Process and
        Protection from Self-Incrimination 132
    Amendment VI: The Right to a Fair Trial 136
    Amendment VII: The Right to a Jury in Civil Cases 139
    Amendment VIII: Protection from Cruel and
        Unusual Punishment 141
    Amendment IX: Rights Beyond the Constitution 143
    Amendment X: States' Rights and Limits of
        Federal Power 144

The Subsequent Amendments............147
  Changing the Constitution........................ 149
  Amendment XI: Limits on Lawsuits Against States........ 151
  Amendment XII: Changing Presidential Elections.........152
  Amendment XIII: Abolishing Slavery 155
  Amendment XIV: Citizenship, Equal Protection,
     and Due Process 157
  Amendment XV: The Right to Vote Regardless of Race... 162
  Amendment XVI: The Federal Income Tax 164
  Amendment XVII: Direct Election of Senators 166
  Amendment XVIII: Prohibition: The Ban on Alcohol 169
  Amendment XIX: The Right to Vote for Women..........172
  Amendment XX: The Lame Duck Amendment...........176
  Amendment XXI: The End of Prohibition 181
  Amendment XXII: Presidential Term Limits............. 184
  Amendment XXIII: Giving Washington, D.C.
     Electoral Votes...................................187
  Amendment XXIV: Banning the Poll Tax 190
  Amendment XXV: Presidential Succession
     and Disability 192
  Amendment XXVI: Lowering the Voting Age to 18........197
  Amendment XXVII: Delaying Congressional
     Pay Raises.....................................200
  Your Rights, Your Voice, Your Future 202

Vote!..................................... 205
  Why Should I Vote?................................206
  Am I Eligible to Vote? 208
  My Voting Checklist 209

Introduction

Why Should We Care About the Constitution?

What if I told you the most important document in the United States was written over 200 years ago and still impacts every text you send, every vote you cast, and every social media post you make?

Let's face it: the U.S. Constitution isn't the kind of thing most people read on a Saturday night. It's full of formal language and rules that can seem disconnected from modern life. But the Constitution isn't just for history class—it's for understanding your life *right now*. Think of it as the ultimate user manual for American government, telling us how to keep things running and protect what matters most. More than two centuries after it was written, it still shapes the rights we have, the laws we follow, and the way our leaders make decisions.

Believe it or not, the Constitution is all about *you*—your rights, your freedoms, and how your voice fits into the bigger picture. Understanding the Constitution is like knowing the rules of a game. If you know the rules, you can tell when someone's breaking them and why it matters. In short: the U.S. Constitution isn't just for lawyers or politicians; it's about real-life issues that affect *you* every day.

The Constitution impacts nearly every part of your daily life, from your right to express yourself freely to the laws that protect you if something goes wrong. Understanding it gives you the tools to not only know your rights but also to defend them when it truly matters.

Decoding Your Rights

This book isn't about memorizing every word of the Constitution or wading through complex legal theories. It's about making sense of it—breaking it down so you can understand what the Constitution really says and why it still matters so much today. Each part of this living document is explained in a way that connects it to life in modern America. You'll also get answers to questions you might hear in the news or even ask yourself, like:

- Can I get in trouble for things I share online?
- Can I get in trouble for criticizing the government?
- Can I wear or say things that show my beliefs, even if other people don't agree?
- What does 'freedom of religion' mean in a country with so many different beliefs?
- Who makes the rules for voting, and why aren't they the same in every state?
- Who decides how our taxes are spent?
- Why do states make their own laws about issues like healthcare and education?
- How are laws even made?
- What can I do if I think a law is unjust?
- What does it mean when a law is 'unconstitutional'?

All these issues are tied to the Constitution. It's a surprisingly broad and powerful document that touches almost every aspect of American life. Whether it's about who has the authority to tax, how laws are challenged in court, what rights you have inside your own home, how we practice our beliefs, or what we can say online, the Constitution is at the heart of it all. So, even if it feels disconnected from daily life, the Constitution is always in the background, defining rights, setting limits, and answering questions we're still asking today.

It's also important to understand that interpreting the Constitution isn't always straightforward. In fact, it's one of the most debated topics in American government. The Supreme Court, the country's highest judicial power, plays a crucial role in this process. Justices on the Supreme Court interpret the Constitution to decide whether laws or actions are "constitutional" (in other words, allowed under the Constitution) and their decisions often have far-reaching effects on our lives. Different people ranging from judges to scholars to politicians can disagree on what the Constitution means, especially when applying it to modern-day issues that the writers of the Constitution couldn't have imagined. This book simplifies the Constitution to help you understand the basics, but keep in mind that there are layers of complexity and ongoing debates that go beyond what we're covering here.

America's First Group Project

The Constitution didn't just appear out of nowhere. After gaining independence from Britain, the United States needed a plan—a solid set of principles to govern the new country without repeating old mistakes like unchecked government power or lack of representation. This led to the Declaration of Independence in 1776, a document that outlined the thirteen colonies' reasons for breaking away from Britain and their vision for a country built on freedom and equality.

But declaring independence from Britain was only the first step. The new states (formerly the colonies) needed a way to work together as a single country, so they created the Articles of Confederation in 1777. The Articles were America's first attempt at a unified government, but they had serious limitations. Under this system, the national (or federal) government had little real authority—it could pass laws but had no power to enforce them, couldn't require states to pay taxes, and struggled to get states to work together. Imagine a group project where no one has the power to make final decisions, and you'll get the idea.

By the 1780s, it was clear the young country needed a stronger, more effective system.

So, in 1787, leaders from each state met in Philadelphia to try again. This time, they aimed for a stronger government that could handle big issues without taking away individual people's freedoms. The result? The Constitution.

It took months of debate and compromise, but the United States Constitution was eventually signed on September 17, 1787, and later ratified—meaning officially approved and put into effect—by the states over the following years.

A Truly Radical Idea

The United States Constitution was one of the most radical documents in history. At a time when most of the world was ruled by kings or an elite class, this document did something unheard of: it put power in the hands of the people. The idea that citizens could have a direct say in their government through voting and participation was truly revolutionary in the eighteenth century. In most of

Europe, ordinary people had little or no role in politics. So a system that allowed citizens to elect their leaders, hold them accountable, and even define their rights was bold and new—and it changed everything.

Even more impressive, the authors of the Constitution (called the "framers") packed all of this into a document just four pages long! (If you want to see those handwritten pages, they're on display at the National Archives in Washington, D.C.) The Constitution is divided into seven Articles (or sections), each one outlining an important part of how the government works. These Articles establish the three branches of government, define state and federal relationships, and create a process for making changes through amendments. Don't worry, we'll break it all down soon!

But the Constitution doesn't just spell out a new government; it introduces a totally different way of distributing power. Instead of handing all authority over to one ruler or group, the framers split the governing power into three branches: the legislative branch (Congress), the executive branch (the President), and the judicial branch (the courts). Each branch has its own powers, and, crucially, each has ways to check the others:

- Congress can *make* laws, but the President has the power to *veto* (or reject) them.
- Courts can *interpret* these laws, but only Congress can *create* them.
- The President can *sign* laws, but the Supreme Court can *overturn* them if they violate the Constitution.
- And if the President or federal judges abuse their power, Congress can *impeach* and *remove* them.

This system of checks and balances was designed to keep any one of the three branches from becoming too powerful, avoiding the kinds of abuses that were common in European monarchies at the time, where many rulers held unchecked authority.

The framers believed the government should work *for* the people. This is what makes the U.S. Constitution (and later a set of amendments called the Bill of Rights) so game-changing: the focus on protecting individual rights. At the time, most governments in the world gave little thought to personal freedoms, and people had almost no legal protection from their rulers. Even today, not all governments guarantee these rights, leaving some people without protection from unfair laws.

The Constitution flips the script by guaranteeing individual rights—like the right to a fair trial and the freedom to speak your mind—even when those in power disagree with you. It also puts limits on the government itself, like giving citizens protection from searches without a warrant and from cruel and unusual punishment. (You'll find plenty more examples of your constitutional rights in the chapters ahead.)

In short, the Constitution wasn't just a new way to run a government—it was a bold experiment in democracy and a revolutionary shift toward legally protecting personal freedom, unlike anything the world had ever seen. Many of the rights and principles it introduced, like the right to vote for our leaders, might seem obvious today, but for people in early America, this system was groundbreaking. It introduced ideas about individual rights, balanced power, and government by the people that went on to inspire other countries around the world.

For example, Norway's 1814 Constitution borrowed ideas straight from the United States to help shape its own government. Mexico's 1824 Constitution also reflected U.S. influence, especially in how it divided power between different branches of government. After World War II, Japan's 1947 Constitution adopted American principles of democracy and human rights. The revolutionary ideas in the U.S. Constitution didn't just change America—they inspired countries across the globe to create fairer systems of their own.

A Living Document

The Constitution was designed to be flexible. In 1787, the United States was still a new country, figuring out how to govern itself after gaining independence from Britain just over ten years earlier. The framers knew they couldn't predict every challenge future generations would face—or even the ones they might deal with in their own time.

To prepare for this, the framers created a government system that could grow and adapt through changes called amendments. Instead of having to rewrite the entire Constitution as the country evolved, amendments could be added to address big issues like ending slavery, expanding voting rights, and protecting new freedoms as they arose. Amendments don't replace the Constitution's original text; instead, they're added at the end to update earlier parts, cancel outdated rules, or create new laws for issues that were never addressed before.

The Constitution's ability to change is one of the reasons it has lasted so long and continues to guide the United States today. Thanks to its adaptable structure, the Constitution has grown along with the nation, allowing it to stay relevant while keeping the original document as the foundation of American government.

The Journey Ahead

For the rest of this book, we'll go through the Constitution step by step. First, we'll break down each part of the main text—the Articles—that set up how the government works. Most Articles are divided into smaller sections that dig into the nitty-gritty details, and we'll unpack those, too. Then we'll dive into the first ten amendments, called the Bill of Rights, and after that, we'll cover the rest of the amendments, which were added from the early 1800s all the way up to 1992.

Each section will cover a different part of the Constitution, from free speech to voting rights to the process of making laws. And instead of just explaining what each section means, we'll dive into why it's relevant now—using real-life examples and stories that show how this old document still impacts your life today.

So, if you're ready to understand the basics of how American government works, what your rights are, and how people can use the Constitution to push for change, you're in the right place. By the end of this book, you'll know your way around the Constitution, how it impacts your life and your family, and, most importantly, how to spot when someone's bending—or breaking—the rules.

Ready to get started? Let's dive into the document that's shaped the United States for over two centuries!

A Note About the Constitution's Wording

All the text of the original Constitution in this book is the exact wording as it was originally written. That means you might notice spelling, punctuation, and grammar that look different from how we write today. Don't worry, though— you don't need to be a legal scholar to follow along. After each excerpt, we'll break it down in simple terms, explain what it means, and explore how it affects you.

The Constitution of the United States of America

THE PREAMBLE

The Preamble is one of the most famous texts in United States history and acts as the Constitution's opening statement. It's a short introduction that explains why the Constitution was written and what the framers wanted to achieve. Think of it as a mission statement for the government. It doesn't give specific powers or rights, but it does outline the main goals and principles the framers believed in. It's a clear and powerful message about creating a government that is fair, protects its people, and supports their well-being and freedom.

Here's the Preamble's full text just as they wrote it:

> "We the People of the United States, in Order to form a more perfect Union, establish Justice, insure domestic Tranquility, provide for the common defence, promote the general Welfare, and secure the Blessings of Liberty to ourselves and our Posterity, do ordain and establish this Constitution for the United States of America."

Let's break this down line by line:

"We the People of the United States": These opening words are powerful because they show that this government is built by the people and for the people. Unlike the British system the United States left behind, where power came from a king, queen, or small ruling group, America's new government was based on the idea that *the people* are in charge, and the government exists with their permission.

"in Order to form a more perfect Union": The framers knew that those Articles of Confederation they wrote back in 1777 hadn't worked very well. They wanted this new government to be stronger, better organized and "more perfect." So this line is all about learning from past mistakes and creating a system that would do a better job uniting the country into a single "Union."

"establish Justice": Justice means fairness, and the framers wanted to make sure the government protected this valuable principle. They wanted laws that were fair, treated everyone equally, and were made in a clear and organized way.

"insure domestic Tranquility": This phrase means making sure there's peace within the country. The framers wanted to avoid conflicts between the states and communities and to maintain a stable government. (If you're wondering why they used "insure" instead of "ensure," you're not alone! "Insure" means to protect against harm, like insurance, while "ensure" means to make sure something happens. So in this case, "insure" refers to protecting national peace and security.)

"provide for the common defence": One of the main reasons for creating a unified government was to protect the country from outside threats. A united nation could defend itself better than a collection of individual states each trying to handle defense on its own.

"promote the general Welfare": This means working toward a strong, stable country where people can thrive. Today, "welfare" often refers to government assistance programs, but in the eighteenth century, it meant something much broader: creating a society that benefits all citizens.

"secure the Blessings of Liberty to ourselves and our Posterity": Liberty, or freedom, was the main reason America fought for independence from Britain. The framers wanted to make sure this freedom was protected, or secure, not just for themselves but also for future generations—what they called "our Posterity."

"do ordain and establish this Constitution for the United States of America.": This final line makes it official. It declares that the people, through their representatives in government, are creating and approving the Constitution as the highest law of the land.

ARTICLE I

The Legislative Branch

The authors of the Constitution wanted to make sure no one person or group could grab too much power. To make this work, they built a system with both separation of powers and balance of powers—two ideas that work together to keep the government fair and functioning. We touched on this in the introduction, but now let's take a closer look at what each one means.

The separation of powers divides the government into three branches, each with its own job. Imagine the U.S. government as a sturdy tree with three large branches growing from the same trunk. Each branch stretches in its own direction, handling different responsibilities, but all three are equally important to the strength of the tree.

The legislative branch (Congress) makes the laws, the executive branch (the President) enforces them, and the judicial branch (the courts) interprets the laws and decides if they follow the Constitution. By keeping these jobs separate, no one branch has control over the entire government.

The balance of powers is about how these branches work together and keep each other in check. No branch can act completely on its own in making major changes to the government. For example, Congress can pass a law, but the President can veto (or reject) it, and the courts can declare it unconstitutional. On the other hand, Congress can override a President's veto, and the Senate must approve judges the President wants to appoint. This system of "checks and balances" makes sure no single branch becomes too powerful and forces them to cooperate when making decisions.

Together, the "separation of powers"—how each branch has its own responsibilities—and the "balance of powers"—how the branches must work with each other—create a government that's both strong and fair, where power is shared and kept under control.

Now that we have a grasp on the overarching structure of the government, let's take a closer look at Congress, which is laid out in Article I of the Constitution. The framers wanted both the people and the states to have a say in how laws are made, so they divided Congress into two parts: the Senate and the House of Representatives. This setup is called a bicameral (meaning "two-room") legislature.

The House represents the people, with the number of Representatives based on a state's population. The Senate, on the other hand, represents all states equally, with each state getting two Senators regardless of its population. This "two-room" system balances the interests of the population and individual states and remains the foundation of how Congress works today.

With this in mind, let's read Article I to see how Congress is organized, why it was designed this way, and what it actually does.

One of the best ways to understand the Constitution's rules is to think of them as answers to specific questions. Each rule was created to solve a problem or explain how something should work. When you recognize what question each part is answering, it becomes easier to see why it matters and how it fits into the larger puzzle of our government. In the following sections, you'll find the original text of each rule, followed by a question-and-answer format to clarify the wording and its meaning.

SECTION 1: THE LAWMAKERS

Article I opens with a simple and direct statement about who should have the power to make laws:

> *"All legislative Powers herein granted shall be vested in a Congress of the United States, which shall consist of a Senate and House of Representatives."*

Simply put, Congress is the only one of the three branches that can create laws for the whole country. Because Congress's power is divided between the Senate and the House of Representatives, both groups must work together to pass new laws.

SECTION 2: THE HOUSE OF REPRESENTATIVES

Section 2 explains how the House of Representatives is set up and how its members are chosen.

How often do we vote for Representatives?

> *"The House of Representatives shall be composed of Members chosen every second Year by the People of the several States..."*

Members of the House of Representatives are elected every two years. The framers wanted House elections to happen often so that Representatives would stay closely connected to the people they serve. If voters aren't happy with their Representative, they don't have to wait long for a new election to replace them.

Who can vote for Representatives?

> *"and the Electors in each State shall have the Qualifications requisite for Electors of the most numerous Branch of the State Legislature."*

This clause says that if you could vote for what your state's largest legislative group was (usually the state's House of Representatives), then you could also vote for members of Congress. But the Constitution didn't set a national rule—each state decided its own voting laws, which often limited voting to white men who owned property. Over time, amendments and federal laws expanded voting rights, and today, all U.S. citizens 18 and older can vote in House elections.

Who can be a Representative?

> *"No person shall be a Representative who shall not have attained to the Age of twenty five Years, and been seven Years a Citizen of the United States, and who shall not, when elected, be an Inhabitant of that State in which he shall be chosen."*

This says that to be a Representative in the House, a person must be at least 25 years old, have been a U.S. citizen for at least seven years, and live in the state they represent (to make sure they have a real connection to the state they serve). These are still the requirements to be a Representative today.

How many Representatives does each state get?

> *"Representatives and direct Taxes shall be apportioned among the several States which may be included within this Union, according to their respective Numbers..."*

The number of Representatives each state has in the House depends on how many people live there. States with more people get more Representatives, while states with fewer people have fewer representatives. This way, states with larger populations have a larger voice in the House, while smaller states still get representation.

How did they count the number of people in each state?

> *"which shall be determined by adding to the whole Number of free Persons, including those bound to Service for a Term of Years, and excluding Indians not taxed, three fifths of all other Persons."*

This quote explains how the original Constitution counted people in each state to determine how many Representatives each state would have in the House. Some of these rules were deeply unfair and do not reflect the values we hold today—but keep reading to see how they have changed over time. Below, we'll break down what each part meant when it was written and how these rules have since been corrected.

"free Persons" were people who were not enslaved and had full rights. They were fully counted in the population.

"those bound to Service for a Term of Years" were people working under a contract for a set period of time, usually to pay off a debt or as part of an agreement to come to the American colonies. These people, called indentured servants, were also fully counted.

"Indians not taxed" meant Native Americans who lived under their own tribal governments and were not counted in the population at all. Since the U.S. government did not consider them part of the country's tax system, they were excluded from the count.

"three fifths of all other Persons" referred to enslaved Black people. Even though each free white person was counted as one person in the population count, each enslaved Black person was counted as only three-fifths (or 60%) of a person. This meant that enslaved Black people weren't given full recognition in the population count.

Southern states, where slavery was common, wanted enslaved Black people to be counted in their population so they could have more seats in the House of Representatives and therefore more power in Congress. However, Northern states disagreed. They didn't want states with large enslaved populations to get extra political power, especially since enslaved people had no rights and couldn't vote. The result was the Three-Fifths Compromise—a political deal that let states with slavery count three-fifths of their enslaved Black people toward their total, giving them more influence in Congress while still denying enslaved people any rights or freedom.

Thankfully, after the Civil War, this part of the Constitution was finally abolished. The Thirteenth Amendment (1865) ended slavery completely, making it illegal in all states. A few years later, the Fourteenth Amendment (1868) ensured that every person was fully counted in the population and granted citizenship to anyone born in the U.S., including formerly enslaved people. The Fifteenth Amendment (1870) protected voting rights for Black men, stating that no one could be denied the right to vote because of "race, color, or previous condition of servitude."

Fifty years later, the Nineteenth Amendment (1920) granted women the right to vote, including Black women. However, it wasn't until the Voting Rights Act of 1965 that racial discrimination in voting was finally outlawed, securing voting rights for Black Americans across the country.

We'll cover these amendments *much* more in the next chapters, but for now, it's important to know that today, the Constitution protects the rights of all people equally, no matter who they are.

How often is the population counted?

> *"The actual Enumeration shall be made within three Years after the first Meeting of the Congress of the United States, and within every subsequent Term of ten Years, in such Manner as they shall by Law direct."*

The Constitution requires a nationwide population count, called the Census, be conducted every ten years. The first was taken in 1790, and it has been held every decade since then to update how many Representatives each state gets.

How many Representatives can there be?

> *"The Number of Representatives shall not exceed one for every thirty Thousand, but each State shall have at Least one Representative…"*

Originally, the Constitution set a limit on how many Representatives there could be: no more than one per 30,000 people. It also guarantees that every state will have at least one Representative, no matter how small their population is. However, as the U.S. population grew, Congress capped the total number of Representatives at 435 in 1929.

As of 2025, the House of Representatives has 435 voting members. California has the most seats (52) because it's the state with the largest population. On the other hand, six states have such small populations that they each have only one Representative: Alaska, Delaware, North Dakota, South Dakota, Vermont, and Wyoming. Instead of representing just one district, these Representatives serve the entire state, a system known as "at-large" representation.

How were the first Representatives divided up?

> "and until such enumeration shall be made, the State of New Hampshire shall be entitled to chuse three, Massachusetts eight, Rhode-Island and Providence Plantations one, Connecticut five, New-York six, New Jersey four, Pennsylvania eight, Delaware one, Maryland six, Virginia ten, North Carolina five, South Carolina five, and Georgia three."

Before the first Census in 1790, the Constitution gave each state a certain number of Representatives based on educated guesses about their populations. These numbers weren't exact, but they were the best estimates available at the time. After the Census officially counted the population a few years later, the number of Representatives for each state was adjusted to match the actual population size.

What happens if a Representative leaves office early?

> *"When vacancies happen in the Representation from any State, the Executive Authority thereof shall issue Writs of Election to fill such Vacancies."*

If a Representative resigns, dies, or leaves office early, the governor of their state (called the "Executive Authority" here) must call a special election to elect a new Representative. This keeps each state fully represented in the House.

Who's the head of the House of Representatives?

> *"The House of Representatives shall chuse their Speaker and other Officers..."*

The House of Representatives elects a leader called the Speaker of the House. The Speaker runs meetings, helps decide which new laws are discussed, and speaks on behalf of the House in important matters. This is a very powerful job in Congress. If the President and Vice President can no longer serve, the Speaker of the House is actually next in line to become President.

What special power does the House have?

> *"and shall have the sole Power of Impeachment."*

The House of Representatives gets a special power called impeachment. This means it's the only part of the government that can officially accuse a government leader—like the President—of serious wrongdoing. Being impeached doesn't kick someone out of office right away. It's more like an official charge, like in a court case, which leads to a trial in the Senate to decide what happens next. This process helps make sure that even powerful leaders must follow the law.

SECTION 3: THE SENATE

Section 3 explains how the Senate is set up and what makes it different from the House of Representatives.

How many Senators does each state get?

> *"The Senate of the United States shall be composed of two Senators from each State..."*

Every state, no matter its size or population, gets exactly two Senators. This is different from the House of Representatives, where the number of Representatives each state has depends on its population. Giving every state an equal number of Senators helps make sure states with fewer people still have a strong voice in the Senate, balancing the influence that very populated states have in the House.

Who picks the Senators?

> *"chosen by the Legislature thereof..."*

Originally, the Constitution said that state legislatures (the people in charge of making *state* laws) were the ones who chose their state's U.S. Senators. This meant that ordinary citizens didn't have a direct say in who represented them in the Senate. But that changed with the Seventeenth Amendment (1913), which gave the power to the people, allowing voters in each state to elect their Senators directly. This new system made the Senate more accountable to the public, and it's still how we elect Senators today.

How long do Senators serve?

"for six Years..."

A Senator's term lasts six years, which is much longer than the two-year terms served by members of the House of Representatives. The framers designed this difference on purpose—while the House was meant to respond quickly to public opinion, the Senate was created to provide stability and long-term decision-making in government.

With six-year terms, Senators can take more time to debate important national issues without the constant pressure of frequent elections. This allows them to focus on crafting policies, reviewing legislation, and advising on major national decisions, rather than always preparing for the next election. However, this also means that if voters are unhappy with a Senator, they have to wait longer to elect someone new.

How many votes does each Senator get?

"and each Senator shall have one Vote."

Each Senator gets one vote, no matter which state they represent. Since every state has two Senators, this ensures that all states have an equal say in the Senate, regardless of population size. This is different from the House of Representatives, where larger states have more votes because they have more Representatives (even though each Representative also gets just one vote).

So the whole Senate changes every six years?

> "Immediately after they shall be assembled in Consequence of the first Election, they shall be divided as equally as may be into three Classes. The Seats of the Senators of the first Class shall be vacated at the Expiration of the second Year, of the second Class at the Expiration of the fourth Year, and of the third Class at the Expiration of the sixth Year, so that one third may be chosen every second Year..."

No. Senators aren't all elected at once. Instead, about one-third of the Senate is up for election every two years. This way, there is always a mix of new members and experienced leaders. It also keeps the government stable by making sure the entire Senate isn't replaced at one time, which could disrupt the government's ability to function smoothly.

What happens if a Senator leaves office early?

> "...and if Vacancies happen by Resignation, or otherwise, during the Recess of the Legislature of any State, the Executive thereof may make temporary Appointments until the next Meeting of the Legislature, which shall then fill such Vacancies."

If a Senator resigns, dies, or leaves office early, the governor of that state (the "Executive") can temporarily appoint a replacement until the state legislature (or today, the voters) elects a new Senator. The rules for filling these vacancies vary by state, and some states require a special election instead of a governor's appointment.

Who can be a Senator?

> *"No Person shall be a Senator who shall not have attained to the Age of thirty Years, and been nine Years a Citizen of the United States, and who shall not, when elected, be an Inhabitant of that State for which he shall be chosen."*

To be a Senator, you have to be at least 30 years old, have been a U.S. citizen for at least nine years, and live in the state you represent. These rules make sure Senators have some experience and know about national issues, while also being connected to the state they serve.

What happens if there's a tie in the Senate?

> *"The Vice President of the United States shall be President of the Senate, but shall have no Vote, unless they be equally divided. The Senate shall chuse their other Officers, and also a President pro tempore, in the Absence of the Vice President, or when he shall exercise the Office of President of the United States."*

The Vice President of the United States also serves as the President of the Senate, but they don't usually vote on new laws. Instead, their most important role in the Senate is breaking a tie. Since the Senate has 100 members—two from each of the 50 states—a 50/50 tie can happen during a vote. When that happens, the Vice President steps in to cast the deciding vote, breaking the tie and determining whether the new law moves forward or fails.

When the Vice President isn't available, the Senate chooses a temporary leader called the President *pro tempore* (which means "for the time being" in Latin). This person is usually the longest-serving Senator from the majority party and helps run Senate meetings.

What is the Senate's role in impeachment?

> *"The Senate shall have the sole Power to try all Impeachments. When sitting for that Purpose, they shall be on Oath or Affirmation. When the President of the United States is tried, the Chief Justice shall preside: And no Person shall be convicted without the Concurrence of two thirds of the Members present."*

If the House of Representatives votes to impeach a government official, like the President, the Senate holds a trial to decide if they should be removed from office. In this trial, Senators act like a jury, listening to evidence and arguments before voting. This rule says that to remove someone from office, at least two-thirds of the Senators must vote guilty. This rule ensures that removing a leader requires strong support from both political parties, not just one side. If the President is on trial, the Chief Justice of the Supreme Court leads the process instead of the Vice President.

What happens when someone is impeached?

> *"Judgment in Cases of Impeachment shall not extend further than to removal from Office, and disqualification to hold and enjoy any Office of honor, Trust or Profit under the United States: but the Party convicted shall nevertheless be liable and subject to Indictment, Trial, Judgment and Punishment, according to Law."*

If convicted in an impeachment trial, a person can only be removed from office and banned from holding another federal position—they cannot be sent to jail as part of the impeachment. They can still be charged with crimes in a regular court and face legal consequences like any other citizen.

SECTION 4: ELECTIONS AND MEETINGS

Section 4 talks about when and how elections and meetings for Congress should happen.

Who decides when elections for Congress are held?

> "The Times, Places and Manner of holding Elections for Senators and Representatives, shall be prescribed in each State by the Legislature thereof; but the Congress may at any time by Law make or alter such Regulations, except as to the Places of chusing Senators."

Each state legislature decides when, where, and how elections for Senators and Representatives are held. This means states set the voting rules, locations, and dates for their own Congressional elections. However, Congress has the power to change these rules if needed—except for the rule that Senators must be chosen from their own state. This allows states to run their own elections while ensuring Congress can step in to make changes if necessary.

When does Congress meet?

> "The Congress shall assemble at least once in every Year, and such Meeting shall be on the first Monday in December, unless they shall by Law appoint a different Day."

Originally, Congress was only required to meet once a year, and that meeting happened on the first Monday in December. But in 1933, the Twentieth Amendment changed things. Now, Congress starts its meetings—or sessions—on January 3rd every odd-numbered year (like 2027, 2029, etc.) and each session of Congress lasts for two years. This two-year period is called a term. So, Congress begins its work on January 3rd of an odd-numbered year, and that group of Senators and Representatives stays in session, working together, until around January 3rd two years later. Then a new Congress begins its own two-year term.

SECTION 5: RULES AND PROCEDURES

Section 5 explains some basic rules for how the House and Senate should run.

Who decides if a member of Congress is qualified?

> *"Each House shall be the Judge of the Elections, Returns and Qualifications of its own Members..."*

Each chamber of Congress—the House of Representatives and the Senate—has the power to decide if its own members were properly elected and meet the qualifications to serve. This means that if there is a dispute about an election, Congress itself—not the courts—makes the final decision on whether someone can take office.

How many members must be present for a vote?

> *"a Majority of each shall constitute a Quorum to do Business..."*

To officially pass laws or make decisions, more than half of the members (a majority) must be present—this is called a quorum. If there aren't enough members in attendance, Congress cannot vote or conduct official business.

What happens if too many members are absent?

> "...but a smaller Number may adjourn from day to day, and may be authorized to compel the Attendance of absent Members, in such Manner, and under such Penalties as each House may provide."

Even if there aren't enough members for a quorum, a smaller group can still meet and force absent members to attend. Congress can even set penalties for members who don't show up when they are supposed to.

Who sets the rules for Congress?

> "Each House may determine the Rules of its Proceedings"

Each chamber of Congress gets to set its own rules for how it operates. This includes deciding how voting works within their chamber, how debates and committees are run, and what the rules of behavior are for their members.

Can Congress discipline its own members?

> "punish its Members for disorderly Behaviour, and, with the Concurrence of two thirds, expel a Member."

Yes, Congress can punish its own members if they break rules or act inappropriately. Members can be reprimanded, fined, or even suspended. If two-thirds of the chamber agrees, a member can be expelled, meaning they are permanently removed from Congress. This helps keep order and maintains a standard of behavior.

How do we know what happens in Congress?

> *"Each House shall keep a Journal of its Proceedings, and from time to time publish the same, excepting such Parts as may in their Judgment require Secrecy…"*

Both the House and Senate must keep an official record of what happens during meetings—this is called a journal. Most of this record is made public, so citizens can see what their representatives are doing. However, Congress can keep certain parts secret if they believe it's necessary.

Can we see how each member of Congress votes?

> *"and the Yeas and Nays of the Members of either House on any question shall, at the Desire of one fifth of those Present, be entered on the Journal."*

Congress records votes, but not every vote is automatically written down. If at least one-fifth of the members present request it, a roll call vote must be recorded in the official journal so the public can see how each member voted. In a roll call vote, each member's name is called, and they must say "yes" ("yea") or "no" ("nay") out loud. This ensures the public can see exactly how each Representative or Senator voted.

Can Congress take long breaks?

> *"Neither House, during the Session of Congress, shall,*

> *without the Consent of the other, adjourn for more than three days..."*

No one chamber of Congress can take a long break by itself. If either the House or Senate wants to pause for more than three days, they need permission from the other chamber.

Can Congress move to a different location?

> *"nor to any other Place than that in which the two Houses shall be sitting."*

Congress can't change locations unless both the House and Senate agree. This rule prevents one chamber from trying to delay work by moving somewhere else.

SECTION 6: PAY AND PROTECTIONS

Section 6 explains how members of Congress are paid and what protections they have while doing their job.

Do members of Congress get paid?

> *"The Senators and Representatives shall receive a Compensation for their Services, to be ascertained by Law..."*

Yes, members of Congress are paid for their work. The amount is set by law, which Congress itself has the power to set. However, to prevent conflicts of interest, the Twenty-Seventh Amendment (1992) now requires that any change to congressional pay can only take effect after the next election, so members of Congress cannot immediately get the pay raises they approve.

What protections do members of Congress have?

> "They shall in all Cases, except Treason, Felony and Breach of the Peace, be privileged from Arrest during their Attendance at the Session of their respective Houses, and in going to and returning from the same..."

Members of Congress have special legal protections to help them do their jobs without interference. While they are attending or traveling to and from Congress, they cannot be arrested for minor offenses like traffic violations or civil disputes. This rule makes sure they can focus on their work without legal distractions or political opponents using the law against them. However, this protection does not apply to serious crimes like treason, felonies, or violent crimes.

Can Congress members be punished for things they say?

> "and for any Speech or Debate in either House, they shall not be questioned in any other Place."

The Constitution also gives members of Congress "speech and debate" immunity, meaning they cannot be punished or sued for things they say during official Congressional debates. This allows lawmakers to speak freely about important issues without fear of being silenced.

Can Congress members have another government job?

> "No Senator or Representative shall, during the Time for which he was elected, be appointed to any civil Office under the Authority of the United States, which

> *shall have been created, or the Emoluments whereof shall have been encreased during such time..."*

Members of Congress cannot take a new federal government job that was created or be given a pay raise while they are serving their elected term in Congress. This rule prevents lawmakers from creating high-paying jobs for themselves or taking advantage of their position to get a new job in the government.

Can someone work for the government and serve in Congress at the same time?

> *" and no Person holding any Office under the United States, shall be a Member of either House during his Continuance in Office."*

If someone already has a federal job—like a judge, military officer, or cabinet member—they cannot also serve in Congress. This rule keeps government powers separate and prevents conflicts of interest, making sure that lawmakers focus on their duties in Congress instead of holding multiple positions at the same time.

SECTION 7: HOW LAWS ARE MADE

Section 7 explains the process of how a proposed idea can become a law.

Who make tax laws?

> *"All Bills for raising Revenue shall originate in the House of Representatives; but the Senate may propose or concur with Amendments as on other Bills."*

A proposal for a new law is called a bill. Any bill that raises revenue—meaning taxes, which are the government's main source of money—must start in the House of Representatives. However, once the House passes the bill, the Senate can suggest changes or approve it.

How does an idea become a law?

> "Every Bill which shall have passed the House of Representatives and the Senate, shall, before it become a Law, be presented to the President of the United States..."

Before a bill can become a law, both the House of Representatives and the Senate must approve it. Then, it goes to the President for final approval.

What can a President do with a bill?

> "If he approve he shall sign it, but if not he shall return it, with his Objections to that House in which it shall have originated, who shall enter the Objections at large on their Journal, and proceed to reconsider it."

The President has two choices when they receive a bill. They can sign it and it becomes a law. Or they can reject it, or veto it. This means they send it back to Congress with a list of reasons why they don't think it should become a law.

Can Congress pass laws without Presidential approval?

> "If after such Reconsideration two thirds of that House shall agree to pass the Bill, it shall be sent, together with the Objections, to the other House, by which it

> shall likewise be reconsidered, and if approved by
> two thirds of that House, it shall become a Law."

If the President vetoes a bill, Congress still has a chance to make the bill a law, but only if two-thirds of both the House and the Senate vote to overrule the President's veto. This system makes sure that the President can't stop a law if it has strong support in Congress.

How do members of the House of Representatives vote?

> "But in all such Cases the Votes of both Houses shall be determined by yeas and Nays, and the Names of the Persons voting for and against the Bill shall be entered on the Journal of each House respectively."

When the House of Representatives votes on a bill, members must say "yea" ("yes") or "nay" ("no"). The names of all members and how they voted are recorded in an official journal, so the public can see how their Representatives voted.

What if the President ignores a bill?

> "If any Bill shall not be returned by the President within ten Days (Sundays excepted) after it shall have been presented to him, the Same shall be a Law, in like Manner as if he had signed it…"

If the President does nothing with a bill for ten days (not counting Sundays), it automatically becomes a law as if the President had signed it.

But what if Congress isn't in session when the President ignores a bill?

> "unless the Congress by their Adjournment prevent its Return, in which Case it shall not be a Law."

If Congress isn't in session and the President doesn't sign the bill within ten days, then it doesn't become law. This is called a "pocket veto," because the President can "pocket" (ignore) the bill, and Congress can't override it.

Do other decisions require the President's approval?

> "Every Order, Resolution, or Vote to which the Concurrence of the Senate and House of Representatives may be necessary (except on a question of Adjournment) shall be presented to the President of the United States..."

Yes! If Congress makes an official decision—like passing a resolution—it usually must be sent to the President for approval, just like a bill. A resolution is a formal statement or decision made by Congress that doesn't necessarily create a new law but can declare a position, set rules for Congress, or propose amendments to the Constitution.

Can Congress override the President's decision?

> "and before the Same shall take Effect, shall be approved by him, or being disapproved by him, shall be repassed by two thirds of the Senate and House of Representatives, according to the Rules and Limitations prescribed in the Case of a Bill."

If the President rejects an official decision, Congress can override the rejection with a two-thirds vote in both the House and the Senate, just like with a vetoed bill.

SECTION 8: THE POWERS OF CONGRESS

Section 8 lists all the powers Congress has to make laws and help run the country. These powers enable Congress to keep the government working, protect the nation, and make sure everything runs smoothly.

How does Congress pay for government programs, like schools and the military?

> *"The Congress shall have Power To lay and collect Taxes, Duties, Imposts and Excises, to pay the Debts and provide for the common Defence and general Welfare of the United States; but all Duties, Imposts and Excises shall be uniform throughout the United States;"*

Congress has the power to collect taxes from people and businesses to pay for important government programs and services. Taxes help fund the military, roads, schools, public safety, and other services that benefit the country. However, there's an important rule: taxes must be the same across the whole country, meaning one state can't be taxed more than another for the same thing. This rule ensures that the government treats all states fairly when collecting money.

What happens if the government runs out of money?

> *"To borrow Money on the credit of the United States;"*

The Constitution gives Congress the power to borrow money when the government doesn't have enough to pay its expenses. When tax money isn't enough, Congress borrows from banks, investors, and even other countries. In return, the government promises to pay the money back later with interest.

Borrowing helps the U.S. pay its bills on time, but if the government borrows too much, it goes into debt. To manage this, Congress sets a debt limit, which is the maximum amount the U.S. can owe. If the government reaches this limit, Congress must decide whether to raise the debt ceiling so borrowing can continue or find other ways to cut spending.

Can Congress control trade?

"To regulate Commerce with foreign Nations, and among the several States, and with the Indian Tribes;"

Congress was given the power to make rules about trade (buying and selling goods) with other countries, trade between states, and trade with Native American tribes. These rules help make sure that businesses follow fair laws and that one state doesn't create different trade rules that might hurt another state. Congress also decides how goods from other countries are taxed and makes trade agreements with other nations.

Who decides how people become U.S. citizens?

"To establish an uniform Rule of Naturalization..."

Congress creates the rules for becoming a U.S. citizen, a process called naturalization. These laws decide who can apply for citizenship, what requirements they must meet, and what steps they need to take. The goal is to make sure the process is fair and the same for everyone, no matter what state they are in. Over time, these laws have changed to reflect different ideas about immigration, but the Constitution gives Congress the power to make and update those laws.

How does Congress help people in debt?

> *"and uniform Laws on the subject of Bankruptcies throughout the United States;"*

Congress also makes laws about bankruptcy, which happens when a person or business can't pay their debts and needs legal help to find a solution. Bankruptcy laws exist to protect both the person in debt and the people or businesses they owe money to. These laws allow people to restart financially while making sure debts are handled fairly. By keeping bankruptcy laws the same in all states, Congress ensures that everyone has the same options and follows the same rules, no matter what state they live in.

Who decides how much a dollar is worth?

> *"To coin Money, regulate the Value thereof, and of foreign Coin, and fix the Standard of Weights and Measures;"*

Congress is the only government branch that has the power to print money. It also decides how much the dollar is worth and makes sure money has a steady value. Without this control, individual states could print their own money, which would cause major economic problems by making the value of money unpredictable.

However, while Congress has the authority, other government agencies help carry out this power. The U.S.

Department of the Treasury oversees the actual printing of paper money and minting of coins, while the Federal Reserve (the U.S. central bank) manages the money supply, controlling how much money is in circulation to help keep the economy balanced.

Congress also makes rules for weights and measurements, so things like miles, pounds, and gallons are the same across the country. This means that when you buy a gallon of milk in one state, it's the exact same size as a gallon in another state. These rules help make trade, science, and everyday life fair and easy to understand.

Can Congress stop people from making fake money?

> *"To provide for the Punishment of counterfeiting the Securities and current Coin of the United States;"*

The Constitution gives Congress the power to make laws to stop people from making fake money, a crime called counterfeiting. Fake money is dangerous because it lowers the value of real money and hurts businesses and the economy. To prevent this, Congress has made counterfeiting a serious crime with heavy fines and long prison sentences.

Who is in charge of the postal system?

> *"To establish Post Offices and post Roads;"*

Congress was put in charge of creating a postal system, making sure people across the country can send and receive mail reliably. This includes setting up post offices, mail routes, and delivery services. Congress also funds postal roads, which were originally built to help mail carriers travel between cities and towns more easily. Today, the United States Postal Service (USPS) is still a government-run agency and Congress oversees its operations and funding. By managing the postal system, Congress helps keep mail affordable, accessible, and secure for everyone, no matter where they live.

How does Congress protect inventors and authors?

> *"To promote the Progress of Science and useful Arts, by securing for limited Times to Authors and Inventors the exclusive Right to their respective Writings and Discoveries;"*

Congress helps inventors and authors by giving them patents and copyrights. A patent protects new inventions, while a copyright protects books, music, and other creative works. These laws allow inventors and creators to own and make money from their ideas for a certain period of time before others can freely use them. This encourages people to create new things, write books, and make discoveries without worrying that someone else will steal their work.

Who has the power to create federal courts?

> *"To constitute Tribunals inferior to the Supreme Court..."*

The power to create courts below the Supreme Court is also granted to Congress. These lower courts, called federal courts, deal with criminal cases, lawsuits, and other legal matters that involve national laws. Without these courts, the Supreme Court would have to handle every case, which would be impossible.

Can Congress make laws about crimes outside the U.S.?

> *"To define and punish Piracies and Felonies committed on the high Seas, and Offences against the Law of Nations..."*

Congress has the power to make laws about crimes that happen in international waters, like piracy (stealing from ships at sea). It can also create laws to punish serious international crimes like human trafficking and terrorism. Since these crimes often happen outside a country's borders or involve multiple nations, the U.S. works with other countries to enforce these laws.

Who can declare war?

> *"To declare War, grant Letters of Marque and Reprisal, and make Rules concerning Captures on Land and Water..."*

Only Congress has the power to declare war. This means the President cannot start a war alone—Congress must approve it first. In fact, the President does not have to agree for Congress to declare war. But once war is officially declared, the President, as Commander in Chief of the military, is responsible for leading and carrying out that war.

Congress also sets rules for war, including what can be done with captured goods and territory from enemy forces. A long time ago, Congress could also give private ship owners permission to attack enemy ships by issuing something called a "Letter of Marque and Reprisal." This was a legal way to turn regular ships into warships. However, this practice is no longer used today.

Who controls the Army?

> *"To raise and support Armies, but no Appropriation of Money to that Use shall be for a longer Term than two Years..."*

The Constitution gave Congress the power to create and fund the U.S. Army, but it could only approve money for two years at a time. This rule was put in place to make sure Congress regularly checks on military spending. It prevents the government from keeping a permanent army without limits and ensures that military spending is controlled.

What about the Navy?

> *"To provide and maintain a Navy..."*

Unlike the Army, the Constitution requires Congress to keep a Navy at all times. This means Congress must make sure the U.S. always has warships ready to protect the country. When the Constitution was written, leaders saw a strong Navy as essential for defending the coastline, protecting trade routes, and responding to threats from other countries. Unlike the Army, which must have its funding reviewed every two years, the Navy is considered a permanent part of national defense. Congress still controls the Navy's budget and can decide how many ships are built and how they are used, but it does not have the power to get rid of the Navy completely.

Who sets the rules for the military?

> *"To make Rules for the Government and Regulation of the land and naval Forces..."*

Congress is in charge of making the rules for the military, including both the Army and the Navy. These rules cover how soldiers and officers should behave, how the military should be organized, and what happens if someone in the military breaks the law. Congress also decides how the military is trained, how promotions work, and what rights service members have.

How did Congress keep the country safe before the U.S. had a full-time military?

> *"To provide for calling forth the Militia to execute the Laws of the Union, suppress Insurrections and repel Invasions..."*

When the Constitution was written, the U.S. did have an Army, but it was much smaller and not always active like today's military. Instead of keeping a large, full-time Army, Congress relied heavily on state militias—groups of ordinary citizens who trained as soldiers and could be called to serve in emergencies. These militias were not part of the regular Army, but Congress had the power to call them into action when needed.

This part of the Constitution gave Congress the power to use "the Militia" for three main reasons: to enforce national laws, stop rebellions (called "insurrections"), and defend the country from invasions.

Today, state militias no longer exist in the same way, and their role has been mostly replaced by the National Guard, which can still be called on by Congress or the President to respond to emergencies, natural disasters, or threats to the country.

Who organized and trained the militias?

> *"To provide for organizing, arming, and disciplining, the Militia, and for governing such Part of them as may be employed in the Service of the United States, reserving to the States respectively, the Appointment of the Officers, and the Authority of training the Militia according to the discipline prescribed by Congress..."*

Congress made the rules for how militias were organized, trained, and armed, but each state was in charge of picking its own officers and running the training. This meant that militias across the country followed the same general rules, but states still had control over how they prepared their soldiers.

Who controls Washington, D.C., since it's not a state?

> *"To exercise exclusive Legislation in all Cases whatsoever, over such District (not exceeding ten Miles square) as may, by Cession of particular States, and the Acceptance of Congress, become the Seat of the Government of the United States..."*

The Constitution established Washington, D.C. as the seat of the federal government and the nation's capital. The framers didn't want the federal government to rely on a state for its headquarters because they worried that could give one state too much influence over national affairs. To prevent this, they created a separate district, independent from any state's control, and gave Congress full authority over it.

Unlike states, which have their own governments to handle local issues, Washington, D.C. is ultimately governed by Congress. While the city has its own local government today, making decisions on many city matters, Congress still has the final say on key aspects of how it is run.

The name District of Columbia comes from Christopher Columbus, whose name was often used as a symbol of America during the country's early years. The word "District" was chosen to emphasize that this land was separate from any state, and the city itself, Washington, was named after George Washington.

Can Congress build military bases?

> *"and to exercise like Authority over all Places purchased by the Consent of the Legislature of the State in which the Same shall be, for the Erection of Forts, Magazines, Arsenals, dock-Yards, and other needful Buildings..."*

Congress has the power to buy land for things like military bases, forts, weapons storage sites (called "magazines"), and shipyards for the Navy. But there's an important rule: the state where the land is located must agree to the purchase. This ensures that states still have a say in how land within their borders is used.

Beyond military sites, this Congressional power also applies to important government buildings, such as courthouses, post offices, and national parks.

What other kinds of laws can Congress pass?

> *"To make all Laws which shall be necessary and proper for carrying into Execution the foregoing Powers,*

and all other Powers vested by this Constitution in the Government of the United States, or in any Department or Officer thereof."

This last line of Section 8 is known as the Necessary and Proper Clause, or sometimes the Elastic Clause because it allows Congress to "stretch" its powers when needed. It gives Congress the flexibility to pass laws that help carry out the powers listed in the Constitution.

For example, the Constitution gives Congress the power to regulate trade, but it doesn't mention anything about the internet or air travel—because neither one existed at the time! However, under the Necessary and Proper Clause, Congress has made laws about both, since they are related to its power over commerce and national security.

SECTION 9: LIMITS ON CONGRESS

While Section 8 explains what Congress *can* do, Section 9 explains what it *can't* do. The framers set these limits to keep the government from becoming too powerful and to protect people's rights and state authority. Some of these rules were important at the time but are now outdated, while others still play a big role in how the government works today.

Let's go through each part of Section 9 and break down what it means.

Did Congress allow the slave trade?

"The Migration or Importation of such Persons as any of the States now existing shall think proper to admit, shall not be prohibited by the Congress prior to the

> *Year one thousand eight hundred and eight, but a Tax or duty may be imposed on such Importation, not exceeding ten dollars for each Person."*

When the Constitution was written in 1787, slavery was still legal in parts of the United States. Some states wanted to end the importation of enslaved Black people, while others wanted to keep it legal. As a compromise, the framers agreed that Congress could not ban the slave trade until 1808. However, the Constitution allowed Congress to place a tax—up to ten dollars per person—on each enslaved person brought into the country.

Once 1808 arrived, Congress passed a law officially banning the importation of enslaved people into the U.S. However, slavery itself was still legal in many states until the Thirteenth Amendment was passed in 1865, abolishing slavery completely.

Can Congress take away our right to a fair trial?

> *"The Privilege of the Writ of Habeas Corpus shall not be suspended, unless when in Cases of Rebellion or Invasion the public Safety may require it."*

No, Congress cannot take away your right to a fair trial, except in extreme cases. The term Habeas Corpus here means that if someone is arrested, they have the right to go in front of a judge and hear the charges against them. This protects people from being thrown in jail without a fair reason or trial.

However, the Constitution allows an exception. If there is a rebellion or invasion, Congress is allowed to temporarily suspend this right to protect public safety. For example, during the Civil War, President Abraham Lincoln suspended Habeas Corpus to stop Confederate supporters from interfering with the war. This decision was controversial, and even today, people debate when—if ever—the government should be allowed to suspend this right.

What kinds of laws can Congress not pass?

> *"No Bill of Attainder or ex post facto Law shall be passed."*

The Constitution clearly states that there are two kinds of unfair laws that Congress is not allowed to pass:

- **A Bill of Attainder:** This is a law that punishes someone without a trial. The Constitution guarantees that everyone gets a fair trial before they can be punished.
- **An Ex Post Facto Law:** This is a law that makes something illegal and then punishes people who did it *before* it was illegal. For example, if Congress passed a law today making it illegal to own a certain type of car, they could not punish people who owned that car last year, when it was still legal.

These rules protect people from unfair punishment and ensure that laws apply fairly to everyone.

How does Congress collect taxes?

> *"No Capitation, or other direct, Tax shall be laid, unless in Proportion to the Census or Enumeration herein before directed to be taken."*

When the Constitution was written, Congress could not collect taxes directly from individual people. Instead,

Congress had to ask each state to pay a share of taxes based on how many people lived there. States with more people had to pay more in taxes, while states with fewer people paid less.

Later, this changed. When we get to the Amendments, you'll see that in 1913, the Sixteenth Amendment gave the government the power to tax people directly, which means that instead of asking states for money, the government now collects taxes straight from people's paychecks or from the money they earn. That's why today, we pay income taxes directly to the federal government, instead of the government going through the states to collect it.

Can Congress tax what states export to other countries?

> *"No Tax or Duty shall be laid on Articles exported from any State."*

Congress cannot tax goods that states export to other countries. This rule was included to make sure that states with large ports, like New York and Virginia, weren't unfairly taxed compared to smaller states. It helped prevent the government from putting a larger tax burden on certain states just because they did more trade with other countries.

Can Congress favor one state's ports over another?

> *"No Preference shall be given by any Regulation of Commerce or Revenue to the Ports of one State over those of another: nor shall Vessels bound to, or from, one State, be obliged to enter, clear, or pay Duties in another."*

This means Congress cannot pass trade laws that favor one state over another. For example, Congress can't create a law that lowers taxes on goods shipped from New York while raising taxes on goods from Virginia. All states must be treated equally in trade and commerce. This rule was meant to keep the federal government from playing favorites, ensuring that every state had a fair chance to grow its economy.

Can the government spend money however it wants?

"No Money shall be drawn from the Treasury, but in Consequence of Appropriations made by Law; and a regular Statement and Account of the Receipts and Expenditures of all public Money shall be published from time to time."

Congress must approve *all* government spending before any money can be taken from the U.S. Treasury. Every dollar spent must be approved by a law passed by Congress. This rule also requires Congress to publish budgets and spending reports so the public can see exactly how tax dollars are being used. This makes sure that citizens can see how the government is using taxpayer money, and hold leaders accountable for how the money is used.

Can the government give people titles of nobility?

"No Title of Nobility shall be granted by the United States: And no Person holding any Office of Profit or Trust under them, shall, without the Consent of the Congress, accept of any present, Emolument, Office, or Title, of any kind whatever, from any King, Prince, or foreign State."

No! The United States was founded on the idea that everyone should be treated equally under the law, not ruled by kings or nobles. That's why the framers made it clear that Congress cannot grant titles of nobility (like "Duke" or "Lord").

This rule also prevents government officials from accepting gifts, payments, or noble titles from foreign governments without approval from Congress. The word "emolument" means any kind of payment, benefit, or gift, so this rule is known as the Emoluments Clause. It was created to prevent corruption and ensure that U.S. leaders serve the American people—not foreign countries trying to buy their influence with money, presents, or special honors.

SECTION 10: LIMITS ON THE STATES

While Section 9 lists what *Congress* cannot do, Section 10 focuses on what *states* cannot do. The framers added these rules to make sure states follow the same basic rules as each other and they don't act like independent countries or pass laws that would weaken the federal government. Some of these limits help keep trade fair between states, while others prevent states from making their own treaties or military decisions.

Let's break down Section 10 down one rule at a time.

Can states act like their own countries?

> "No State shall enter into any Treaty, Alliance, or Confederation; grant Letters of Marque and Reprisal; coin Money; emit Bills of Credit; make any Thing but gold and silver Coin a Tender in Payment of Debts;

> *pass any Bill of Attainder, ex post facto Law, or Law impairing the Obligation of Contracts, or grant any Title of Nobility."*

This rule prevents states from making treaties with foreign countries, forming alliances, or creating their own money. In other words, states cannot act like independent nations. The framers wanted the United States to be one unified country, not a group of separate states with different currencies and foreign policies.

This section also stops states from passing the same kinds of unfair laws that Congress is prohibited from passing. These rules help ensure laws are fair and predictable across the country. They include:

- **Bills of Attainder:** When the government punishes people without a trial.
- **Ex Post Facto Laws:** When a law makes something illegal and punishes people for doing it before it was against the law.
- **Laws that weaken contracts:** When the government cancels or changes legal agreements, like contracts, that were already made.
- **Titles of Nobility:** When the state grants people noble or royal titles.

Can states collect their own import taxes?

> *"No State shall, without the Consent of the Congress, lay any Imposts or Duties on Imports or Exports, except what may be absolutely necessary for executing its inspection Laws; and the net Produce of all Duties and Imposts, laid by any State on Imports*

> or Exports, shall be for the Use of the Treasury of the United States; and all such Laws shall be subject to the Revision and Control of the Congress."

The Constitution makes it clear that states cannot charge their own taxes ("imposts or duties") on goods imported from other countries without Congress's approval. The framers included this rule to keep trade fair and consistent across all states. If states could set their own import taxes, they might try to charge extra fees on products coming from other states or foreign countries, making trade more expensive and complicated.

There is one small exception: states can charge fees for inspecting goods (like checking food safety or making sure products meet legal standards). However, any money collected from these fees must go to the U.S. Treasury. Congress is also given the power to review or change these rules.

Could a state create its own army? Or start a war?

> "No State shall, without the Consent of Congress, lay any Duty of Tonnage, keep Troops, or Ships of War in time of Peace, enter into any Agreement or Compact with another State, or with a foreign Power, or engage in War, unless actually invaded, or in such imminent Danger as will not admit of delay."

States cannot have their own armies, warships, or military agreements unless Congress approves. The framers wanted to make sure the federal government controlled national defense, rather than having each state control its own military like in the very early days of the country.

However, if a state is being invaded or facing an immediate attack, it can act to defend itself without waiting for the approval of Congress. This makes sure that states can protect their people in emergencies, but they cannot start wars or make military decisions on their own.

ARTICLE II

The Executive Branch

Article II explains the rules for the executive branch of the U.S. government, which is led by the President. While Congress makes the laws, the President's job to make sure they're carried out. But enforcing laws is only part of what the President does. As the leader of the country, the President makes big decisions that affect all Americans and represents the United States to the rest of the world. This includes building relationships with other countries, negotiating treaties (with approval from the Senate), and speaking on behalf of the United States.

The President is also the Commander in Chief of the armed forces, meaning they're in charge of the military. They make key decisions about defense and national security to keep the country safe, although remember that only Congress has the power to officially declare war.

In addition to working with Congress on laws—by signing or vetoing bills—the President also appoints important government leaders, such as Supreme Court justices and Cabinet members, who help manage different parts of the government. The Cabinet is a group of advisors chosen by the President to lead major government departments, like education, defense, and transportation. Each Cabinet member is in charge of a specific area of government and helps the President make decisions on important national issues.

In short, the President's job is to keep the government running smoothly, protect the country, and represent the U.S. at home and abroad.

Now, let's go through Article II section by section to understand how the executive branch is organized and what powers and responsibilities the President has.

SECTION 1: THE PRESIDENT AND VICE PRESIDENT

Article II, Section 1 explains how the President is elected, who can serve as President, what happens if they can't continue in office, and how they are paid. This section also introduces the position of Vice President, who is next in line if the President cannot serve.

What is the executive branch?

> *"The executive Power shall be vested in a President of the United States of America. He shall hold his Office during the Term of four Years, and, together with the Vice President, chosen for the same Term, be elected, as follows..."*

This says that the executive branch of the United States government is led by the President, whose job is to enforce the laws passed by Congress. The President serves a term of four years, along with the Vice President, who is elected for the same time period.

How is the President elected?

> *"Each State shall appoint, in such Manner as the Legislature thereof may direct, a Number of Electors..."*

When you vote for President, you might think your vote alone decides who wins. But unlike Senators and members of the House of Representatives, the President is not actually elected directly by the people. Instead, the President is chosen by electors through a system called the Electoral College.

How does the Electoral College work?

The Electoral College can be difficult to understand, and many Americans find it confusing. Since it's so fundamental to our democracy, let's take this opportunity to explain exactly how it works, step by step. Once you understand it, you'll get to read the original words from the Constitution, just as the framers wrote them.

Each state gets a certain number of electors.
- The number of electors a state has is based on how many Senators and Representatives it has in Congress.
- Every state has two Senators, plus at least one Representative, so the states with the fewest people will always have a minimum of three electors.
- States with larger populations have more electors because they have more Representatives in Congress. Every 10 years, when the Census counts the U.S. population, the number of Representatives can change, which means a state's electoral votes may also increase or decrease. As of the 2020 Census, the two states with the most electors are California (54) and Texas (40).

Electors cannot be government officials.
- The Constitution says that electors cannot be Senators, Representatives, or federal government employees. This rule prevents people with federal power from having influence over the election.

People vote, but electors cast the official votes.
- When Americans go to the polls every four years in November, they aren't directly voting for President—they're voting for a set of electors who have promised to vote for a specific candidate.
- In most states, the Presidential candidate who wins the most votes in that state receives *all* of its electoral votes. This system is called "winner-takes-all." However, Maine and Nebraska use a different method called the Congressional District Method. In these states, each Congressional District awards one electoral vote to the candidate who wins that district, while the remaining two electoral votes (representing the state's two Senators) go to the candidate who wins the statewide popular vote.

Electors officially vote in December.
- After the election, the electors from each state meet in their state capitals and cast their official votes.
- Instead of casting two votes for President, as you might recall that the original Constitution required, today each elector casts one vote for President and one vote for Vice President. This change was made in 1804 by the Twelfth Amendment, so you'll learn a lot more about the reasons later.
- The electors write down their votes, sign them, and send them in a sealed envelope to Washington, D.C.

Congress counts the votes.
- The sealed votes are sent to the President of the Senate, who is the Vice President of the United States.
- In January, the Senate and House of Representatives meet together, and the Vice President opens the envelopes and reads the results out loud.

Whoever gets the majority of electoral votes wins.
- To win the Presidency, a candidate must get more than half of the total electoral votes.
- As of the 2020 Census, there are 538 electors, so a candidate needs at least 270 votes to win.

What if there's a tie for President?

If no candidate gets a majority, the House of Representatives chooses the President from the top three candidates. In this case, instead of each Representative getting a vote, each state gets one vote. A candidate must win a majority of states to become President.

What if there's a tie for Vice President?
- If the Vice President's race is tied, the Senate chooses the winner. This rare event has only happened once in U.S. history, in 1836.

Congress sets the election schedule.
- The Constitution gives Congress the power to decide when elections happen. Today, the Presidential election takes place on the first Tuesday of November, and electors vote in December.

Why is the Electoral College so complicated?

You might be wondering the same thing many people ask: why we don't just count every citizen's vote equally and let the person with the most votes win?

Well, the Electoral College was created as a compromise between letting Congress choose the President and letting all citizens vote directly.

Some people like the Electoral College system because it gives smaller states a bigger voice in elections. Others don't like it because a candidate can win the Presidency without winning the most individual votes nationwide. It's one of the most unique parts of U.S. elections, and people still debate today whether it's fair or if it should be changed.

Now that you understand how the Electoral College works, read the exact wording from the Constitution:

> "The Electors shall meet in their respective States, and vote by Ballot for two Persons, of whom one at least shall not be an Inhabitant of the same State with themselves. And they shall make a List of all the Persons voted for, and of the Number of Votes for each; which List they shall sign and certify, and transmit sealed to the Seat of the Government of the United States, directed to the President of the Senate. The President of the Senate shall, in the Presence of the Senate and House of Representatives, open all the Certificates, and the Votes shall then be counted. The Person having the greatest Number of Votes shall be the President, if such Number be a Majority of the whole Number of Electors appointed; and if there be more than one who have such Majority, and have an equal Number of Votes, then the House of Representatives shall immediately chuse by Ballot one of them for President; and if no Person have a Majority, then from the five highest on the List the said House shall in like Manner chuse the President. But in chusing the President, the Votes shall be taken by States, the Representation from each State having one Vote; A quorum for this Purpose shall consist of a Member or Members from two thirds of the States, and a Majority of all the

States shall be necessary to a Choice. In every Case, after the Choice of the President, the Person having the greatest Number of Votes of the Electors shall be the Vice President. But if there should remain two or more who have equal Votes, the Senate shall chuse from them by Ballot the Vice President.

"The Congress may determine the Time of chusing the Electors, and the Day on which they shall give their Votes; which Day shall be the same throughout the United States."

Who can be President?

"No Person except a natural born Citizen, or a Citizen of the United States, at the time of the Adoption of this Constitution, shall be eligible to the Office of President; neither shall any Person be eligible to that Office who shall not have attained to the Age of thirty five Years, and been fourteen Years a Resident within the United States."

This says that to become President, a person has to meet both these requirements.

1. They must be a natural-born citizen of the United States, which simply means that they were born a U.S. citizen—they didn't become one later in life. This can happen in a couple of ways:
   - They were born in the United States (or its territories) or on U.S. soil, even if their parents aren't citizens.
   - They were born outside the U.S. and at least one of their parents is a U.S. citizen.
2. A person must also be at least 35 years old and have lived in the United States for at least 14 years.

These rules were put in place to make sure that Presidents have strong ties to the country and enough experience to handle the responsibilities of the office.

What happens if the President can't serve?

> *"In Case of the Removal of the President from Office, or of his Death, Resignation, or Inability to discharge the Powers and Duties of the said Office, the Same shall devolve on the Vice President, and the Congress may by Law provide for the Case of Removal, Death, Resignation or Inability, both of the President and Vice President, declaring what Officer shall then act as President, and such Officer shall act accordingly, until the Disability be removed, or a President shall be elected."*

If the President can't continue in office—whether it's because of illness, death, resignation, or is removed from office—the Vice President takes over. The framers also gave Congress the power to pass laws deciding who will take over if *both* the President and Vice President are unable to serve.

Does the President get paid?

> *"The President shall, at stated Times, receive for his Services, a Compensation, which shall neither be encreased nor diminished during the Period for which he shall have been elected, and he shall not receive within that Period any other Emolument from the United States, or any of them."*

Yes, the President receives a salary. Congress sets the salary before a Presidential term begins and it cannot be changed while the President is in office. Also, the President cannot accept extra money, gifts, or other payments from the U.S. or any state.

What oath does the President take?

> *"Before he enter on the Execution of his Office, he shall take the following Oath or Affirmation:—"I do solemnly swear (or affirm) that I will faithfully execute the Office of President of the United States, and will to the best of my Ability, preserve, protect and defend the Constitution of the United States."*

Before taking office, the President must take an oath of office, promising to carry out the laws and defend the Constitution. This oath is a powerful reminder that the President's job is to serve the country and uphold its laws. Fun fact: the oath has stayed exactly the same since it was first written—and every U.S. President has taken it, starting with George Washington in 1789.

SECTION 2: POWERS OF THE PRESIDENT

Article II, Section 2 explains what powers the President has. This section lays out the President's role as Commander in Chief, their power to make treaties and appoint leaders, and their ability to pardon people who have broken federal laws.

What is the President's role in the military?

> *"The President shall be Commander in Chief of the Army and Navy of the United States, and of the Militia of the several States, when called into the actual Service of the United States…"*

The President is the Commander in Chief of the United States military, meaning they are in charge of the Army, Navy, Air Force, Marines, and Coast Guard. This gives the President a huge responsibility in protecting the country. Remember from Article I, though, that only Congress has the power to declare war, so even as Commander in Chief, a President cannot start wars on their own.

Can the President get help from advisors?

> *"he may require the Opinion, in writing, of the principal Officer in each of the executive Departments, upon any Subject relating to the Duties of their respective Offices..."*

Presidents don't make every decision alone. They have a team of advisors called the Cabinet, made up of the heads of major government departments like defense, education, and transportation. These leaders give the President expert advice on their areas. For example, the Secretary of Defense advises on military matters, the Secretary of State helps with relations between the U.S. and other countries, and the Secretary of the Treasury manages the country's money and economy. Even though Presidents have the final say, they rely on Cabinet members for important decisions.

Can the President let someone out of jail?

> *"and he shall have Power to grant Reprieves and Pardons for Offences against the United States, except in Cases of Impeachment."*

Yes, the President has the power to pardon (forgive) people who have been convicted of federal crimes. A pardon removes the person's punishment, including prison time or fines they have to pay, and gives them back their civil rights, such as the right to vote. However, this power has important limits:

- The President can only pardon federal crimes. If someone is convicted under state law, only the governor of that state can pardon them.
- The President cannot undo an impeachment. If a President, judge, or other government official is impeached by Congress, the President cannot use a pardon to remove the consequences.

Presidents often give many pardons at the end of their time in office, usually to help people they believe were treated unfairly by the justice system or to correct past injustices.

Can the President make treaties with other countries?

"He shall have Power, by and with the Advice and Consent of the Senate, to make Treaties, provided two thirds of the Senators present concur..."

Presidents can make treaties, which are official agreements with other countries, but they cannot do it alone. The Senate has to approve a treaty with a two-thirds majority vote before it becomes official. This keeps the President from making binding agreements with other countries without approval of another branch of government.

Treaties are used for many reasons, such as peace agreements between countries, trade deals that help the economy, and military alliances. For example, the United States is part of NATO, a treaty where countries agree to protect each other if one is attacked.

Who does the President get to appoint?

> "and he shall nominate, and by and with the Advice and Consent of the Senate, shall appoint Ambassadors, other public Ministers and Consuls, Judges of the supreme Court, and all other Officers of the United States, whose Appointments are not herein otherwise provided for, and which shall be established by Law..."

The President chooses (or appoints) many important government leaders, including ambassadors (who represent the U.S. in other countries), Supreme Court justices (the highest judges in the country), and Cabinet members (who help run different parts of the government).

However, as with so many decisions, the President does not have the final say—the Senate must approve these "appointments" before they take effect. For example, if a Supreme Court Justice retires, the President picks a replacement, but the Senate must vote to approve them before they can start the job.

Can the President hire people without Senate approval?

> "but the Congress may by Law vest the Appointment of such inferior Officers, as they think proper, in the President alone, in the Courts of Law, or in the Heads of Departments."

The Constitution says Congress can allow the President to appoint certain lower-level government officials without Senate approval. These positions are usually ones that do not have long terms or the power to create policies, but they are still important for carrying out government operations.

For example, the President can directly appoint White House staff, military officers, and some federal agency officials. However, not all agency heads are included. Important jobs like the FBI Director or CIA Director still need Senate confirmation.

What if the Senate is on break when an important person is hired?

> *"The President shall have Power to fill up all Vacancies that may happen during the Recess of the Senate, by granting Commissions which shall expire at the End of their next Session."*

If a government position becomes empty while the Senate is not in session, the President can temporarily fill the position without waiting for Senate approval. But this is only a temporary fix. When the Senate returns, they still have to vote on whether to approve the person for the job.

SECTION 3: DUTIES OF THE PRESIDENT

Article II, Section 3 explains what the President must do to keep the government running smoothly. While Section 2 listed the President's *powers*, this section focuses on the President's *responsibilities*, or the things they are required to do as the leader of the country.

Does the President report to Congress?

> *"He shall from time to time give to the Congress Information of the State of the Union, and recommend to their Consideration such Measures as he shall judge necessary and expedient..."*

Every year, the President gives the State of the Union Address, a speech about how things are going in the country, and discusses important issues. The Constitution says the President has to give this update "to the Congress," but over time, it has become a televised speech for the entire nation to watch. This allows the President to speak directly to the American people. It's a chance to talk about what has happened over the past year, discuss the country's progress, and share their goals and plans for the future. The President can also propose new laws or policies that they believe would benefit the country.

Can the President call Congress back from recess?

> *"He may, on extraordinary Occasions, convene both Houses, or either of them..."*

If an urgent issue arises while Congress is on break, the President has the power to call them back into session. This ensures that important laws or national emergencies can be addressed quickly. This power has been used in the past, such as when President Harry Truman called Congress back in 1948 to deal with economic issues after World War II.

Can the President dismiss Congress?

> *"and in Case of Disagreement between them, with Respect to the Time of Adjournment, he may adjourn them to such Time as he shall think proper."*

The President also has a very rare power to adjourn Congress (meaning, end a session) if the House and Senate cannot agree on when to end it. However, this power has never been used in U.S. history.

What role does the President play in foreign relations?

"He shall receive Ambassadors and other public Ministers."

The President represents the United States in meetings with foreign governments. By hosting ambassadors from other countries, the President officially recognizes those nations and helps maintain relationships with them. This is an important part of diplomacy, which means working with other countries to solve problems, make trade agreements, keep peace, and strengthen international partnerships.

What if the President doesn't agree with a law?

"He shall take Care that the Laws be faithfully executed."

The President has the duty—as stated in his oath of office—to make sure all laws passed by Congress are "faithfully executed" (enforced). The President can't ignore laws they don't like or choose which ones to follow. In fact, this role as the enforcer of laws is one of the President's most important responsibilities.

To perform this duty, the President oversees government departments and agencies that turn laws into action. These agencies handle the day-to-day work of making sure that the laws passed by Congress actually affect people's lives. The President's job is to make sure they are doing their work effectively.

For example, the Department of Education enforces laws about schools and student rights, while the Department of Defense makes sure national security laws are followed.

Agencies like the Environmental Protection Agency enforce environmental laws, such as those protecting clean air and water.

Who makes a government job official?

> *"and shall Commission all the Officers of the United States."*

When someone gets an important government job, like a general in the military, a federal judge, or an ambassador, the President has to make it official by signing a document called a commission. Think of it like when you win a contest but it doesn't feel official until they hand you the certificate. That's what the President does for people in important jobs. Congress will approve someone for the job, but they can't start until the President signs their commission.

SECTION 4: IMPEACHMENT OF THE PRESIDENT

The President is one of the most powerful people in the country, but they have to follow the law just like everyone else. The framers knew that if a President commits serious crimes or abuses their power, there must be a way to remove them from office. Article II, Section 4 of the Constitution is short and direct in explaining how this works.

Can the President be removed from office?

> *"The President, Vice President and all civil Officers of the United States, shall be removed from Office on Impeachment for, and Conviction of, Treason, Bribery, or other high Crimes and Misdemeanors."*

Yes, a President, Vice President, or other government official can be impeached and forced to leave office if they're convicted of serious crimes. The impeachment process ensures even the highest leaders in the U.S. must follow the law and can be removed from power if they abuse their position. The Constitution lists these reasons for impeachment:

- **"Treason"** means betraying the country, such as helping an enemy during war, spying for another nation, or trying to overthrow the U.S. government. It will be discussed a lot more in Article III, Section 3.
- **"Bribery"** is when someone offers or accepts money, gifts, or favors in exchange for doing something dishonest or unfair. For example, if a government leader takes money from a company and then changes a law to help that company, that would be bribery.
- **"High Crimes and Misdemeanors"** is a broader term that includes breaking the law while in office and other serious abuses of power. It's up to Congress to decide what crimes or misconduct are an impeachable offense.

We already saw in Article I, Sections 2 and 3 how impeachment works in Congress. So, you'll remember that being impeached does not automatically mean a President leaves office. First, the House of Representatives must vote to impeach the President. Then, the Senate holds a trial to decide if the President is guilty. If two-thirds of Senators votes to convict, only then is the President removed from office. As of 2024, this process has only happened four times in U.S. history: President Andrew Johnson in 1868, President Bill Clinton in 1998, and President Donald Trump in 2019 and 2021. The House impeached all three Presidents, but the Senate did not convict them, so they stayed in office.

ARTICLE III

The Judicial Branch

Article III sets up the judicial branch of the U.S. government, which includes the Supreme Court and other federal courts. These courts interpret the laws and decide if they are in line with the framework of the Constitution. Their job is to make sure that the government protects people's rights and follows its own rules.

SECTION 1: THE SUPREME COURT & FEDERAL COURTS

How are courts organized in the U.S.?

> *"The judicial Power of the United States, shall be vested in one supreme Court, and in such inferior Courts as the Congress may from time to time ordain and establish."*

This rule creates a court system for the United States, which is divided into levels of power, like a pyramid. At the very top is the Supreme Court, the highest court in the country. It has the final say on cases related to the Constitution, as well as cases where lower courts disagree. The Supreme Court's decisions are binding on the entire country, which means they apply to all states and all people.

Below the Supreme Court is a system of federal courts. The word "federal" means these courts are part of the national (federal) government, not controlled by individual states. So federal courts handle cases involving national laws, disputes between states, or issues that affect the whole country.

At the bottom of the pyramid are state courts, which are not part of the federal judicial branch and are not mentioned in this section of the Constitution. However, they are important to know about because they handle most everyday cases, such as crimes, traffic violations, and family law matters. Each state has its own court system, and most legal cases in the U.S. start and end in state courts. Sometimes, though, a case that starts in state court can move up to the federal court system if it involves federal law or the Constitution. In rare cases, it can even reach the Supreme Court, which makes the final ruling.

How long do federal judges serve?

> *"The Judges, both of the supreme and inferior Courts, shall hold their Offices during good Behaviour..."*

Judges on the Supreme Court and other federal courts can serve for life, as long as they have "good behavior." By this, the framers mean that they can keep their jobs as long as they follow the law and do their work responsibly. Unlike elected officials, federal judges do not have to run for re-election or worry about losing their job because of political pressure. This rule helps protect federal judges from giving in to outside pressures, so they will make fair decisions—even if those decisions are unpopular—without worrying they could lose their jobs.

Do federal judges get paid?

> *"and shall, at stated Times, receive for their Services, a Compensation, which shall not be diminished during their Continuance in Office."*

Yes, federal judges get paid for their work, and their salary can't be lowered while they're in office. This rule is important because it also protects judges from political pressure. It makes sure they don't have to worry about losing money for making decisions that some people don't like. For example, if Congress disagrees with a judge's rulings, they cannot punish the judge by cutting their pay.

SECTION 2: POWERS OF THE FEDERAL COURTS

Article III, Section 2 explains what kinds of cases federal courts can hear and what role the Supreme Court plays. It also explains the types of authority courts have and guarantees people the right to a jury trial in most criminal cases.

What cases do federal courts handle?

> *"The judicial Power shall extend to all Cases, in Law and Equity, arising under this Constitution, the Laws of the United States, and Treaties made, or which shall be made, under their Authority;—to all Cases affecting Ambassadors, other public Ministers and Consuls;—to all Cases of admiralty and maritime Jurisdiction;—to Controversies to which the United States shall be a Party;—to Controversies between two or more States;— between a State and Citizens of another State,—between Citizens of different States,—between Citizens of the same State claiming Lands under Grants of different States, and between a State, or the Citizens thereof, and foreign States, Citizens or Subjects."*

This rule makes it clear that national issues are decided in federal courts. (Local and state issues are handled by state courts.) Federal laws apply to *everyone* in the U.S., no matter what state they live in. Because of this, federal courts rule on big cases such as:

- Disputes between states
- Cases involving the U.S. government
- Disagreements about Constitutional rights
- Lawsuits between people from different states
- Legal issues with ambassadors or foreign governments (like treaties)
- Cases related to the ocean (called maritime law)

Why do some cases go directly to the Supreme Court?

> *"In all Cases affecting Ambassadors, other public Ministers and Consuls, and those in which a State shall be Party, the supreme Court shall have original Jurisdiction."*

Jurisdiction is the power a court has to hear and rule on certain types of cases. This rule states that the Supreme Court has "original jurisdiction" over some types of cases, meaning it hears these cases right away, without them going through lower courts first. The Constitution gives the Supreme Court original jurisdiction on very important cases, like ones involving ambassadors or arguments between states. Because these issues can have major national and international impact, the Constitution allows the Supreme Court to handle them right from the start.

Does the Supreme Court hear appeals?

> *"In all the other Cases before mentioned, the supreme Court shall have appellate Jurisdiction, both*

> *as to Law and Fact, with such Exceptions, and under such Regulations as the Congress shall make."*

Most of the time, the Supreme Court isn't the first court to hear a case. Instead of original jurisdiction, it has appellate jurisdiction, which means it reviews cases that have already been decided by courts lower down on the pyramid.

If someone disagrees with a lower court's decision, they can file an appeal—a request for a court higher up on the pyramid to look at the case again. In these appeals, the Supreme Court does not hold a new trial. Instead, it reviews how the lower court followed the law to decide if it was done correctly. This is how the Supreme Court handles most of its cases. It allows the Supreme Court to make sure laws are applied fairly across the country and to resolve disagreements between lower courts.

Who has the right to a jury trial?

> *"The Trial of all Crimes, except in Cases of Impeachment, shall be by Jury;"*

The Constitution promises the right to a trial by jury for almost all criminal trials. This means that instead of a judge alone deciding if someone is guilty or innocent, a jury (a group of ordinary citizens) listens to the evidence and makes the decision. This rule is designed to make trials fair by ensuring that a person is judged by their peers—other people like them—rather than just a government official. The only exception to this rule is impeachment trials, which we have learned are handled by the Senate instead of a jury.

Where do trials take place?

> *"and such Trial shall be held in the State where the said Crimes shall have been committed; but when not committed within any State, the Trial shall be at such Place or Places as the Congress may by Law have directed."*

This says that if a crime happens within a state, the trial must take place in that state. But if the crime happens outside a state's borders, such as in U.S. territories, on international waters, or in Washington, D.C., then Congress decides where the trial will take place.

SECTION 3: TREASON

Article III, Section 3 defines treason, the most serious crime against the United States. It also explains how someone can be convicted of treason and what punishment they might face. By including clear rules, the Constitution makes sure that treason charges are only used for truly serious crimes and that no one can be convicted without strong evidence.

What is treason?

> *"Treason against the United States, shall consist only in levying War against them, or in adhering to their Enemies, giving them Aid and Comfort."*

Treason is when a citizen betrays their country, in this case, the United States. The Constitution gives a very specific definition of treason. A U.S. citizen commits treason if they:

- Start a war against the U.S.
- Help the country's enemies by giving them weapons, money, or other support.

The framers made sure this definition was strict and limited because, in the past, some governments wrongly accused people of treason just for disagreeing with those in power.

By keeping the definition clear, the Constitution ensures that treason only applies to truly serious acts of betrayal—especially since, as you will learn, the punishment for treason is extremely serious.

How can someone be convicted of treason?

> *"No Person shall be convicted of Treason unless on the Testimony of two Witnesses to the same overt Act, or on Confession in open Court."*

To be convicted of treason, this says, there must be clear and strong evidence. The Constitution requires the testimony of at least "two witnesses" who saw the crime happen, or, the person must confess "in open court." In other words, a single person's accusation is not enough to convict someone of treason. This rule makes it hard to accuse someone of treason without strong proof, which helps protect people from being falsely accused.

What is the punishment for treason?

> *"The Congress shall have Power to declare the Punishment of Treason, but no Attainder of Treason shall work Corruption of Blood, or Forfeiture except during the Life of the Person attainted."*

The Constitution gives Congress the power to decide how treason is punished. In the past, people convicted of treason in the U.S. have faced either the death penalty or long prison sentences. Today, the most common punishment is life in prison. Treason is still a federal crime today, meaning the death penalty remains a legal option, even though many individual states have banned it.

The Constitution places an important limit on this punishment. If someone is convicted of treason, their family cannot also be punished for their crime. This is what is meant by "no Attainder of Treason shall work Corruption of Blood." While this may seem obvious today, in older times, some governments punished not just the traitor but also their entire family, often taking away their land and property. The framers of the Constitution wanted to prevent this kind of unfair punishment, ensuring that a treason conviction only affects the person guilty of the crime, not their relatives, too.

ARTICLE IV

How States Work Together

Article IV explains how states should cooperate with each other and the federal government. It covers things like how states should respect each other's laws, how new states can join the country, and what the federal government promises to do for each state. Let's go through each part to see what it all means.

SECTION 1: RESPECTING OTHER STATES' LAWS

How should states treat each other's laws?

> *"Full Faith and Credit shall be given in each State to the public Acts, Records, and judicial Proceedings of every other State. And the Congress may by general Laws prescribe the Manner in which such Acts, Records and Proceedings shall be proved, and the Effect thereof."*

The Constitution says that every state must respect the laws, records (official documents issued by a state, such as birth certificates), and court decisions of other states. This rule, called Full Faith and Credit, helps keep things fair and consistent across the country. It ensures that while states have the power to make their own laws, they still have to recognize legal decisions made in other states.

For example, if you get a driver's license in one state, every other state is required to accept it. The same applies to things like marriage licenses and legal name changes—you don't have to redo them just because you move to a new state.

But this rule doesn't cover everything. Some things—like a license to practice as a doctor, lawyer, or teacher—do not automatically transfer between states. That's because each state has its own requirements for these types of jobs to make sure professionals meet local standards.

The second part of this rule lets Congress make laws to explain how states should accept and use each other's official records and court decisions. This means Congress can create clear rules to make sure all states follow the same process when recognizing each other's documents and legal rulings.

SECTION 2: RESPONSIBILITIES BETWEEN STATES

Section 2 explains how states must treat citizens from other states and work together when handling legal matters.

Do citizens have the same rights in every state?

> *"The Citizens of each State shall be entitled to all Privileges and Immunities of Citizens in the several States."*

When the framers wrote this section, they wanted to make sure people wouldn't be treated unfairly in one state just because they were from a different state. Their goal was to create a fair system where all citizens had certain basic rights, no matter where they traveled or moved within the country.

Even though this rule was meant to make sure that all American citizens had the same "privileges," state laws can still be different. For example, minimum wage laws vary between states, meaning workers in some places earn less for the same job. Access to healthcare also differs, with some states offering more services than others. Education systems aren't the same everywhere either, as some states provide more funding to schools or have different graduation requirements. Because of these differences, not everyone today feels they have the same opportunities and benefits across the country.

What if someone breaks the law and flees to another state?

> *"A Person charged in any State with Treason, Felony, or other Crime, who shall flee from Justice, and be found in another State, shall on Demand of the executive Authority of the State from which he fled, be delivered up, to be removed to the State having Jurisdiction of the Crime."*

If someone commits a crime in one state and runs away to another state, they can't escape punishment just by leaving. This rule, called extradition, allows the state where the crime happened to ask for the person to be sent back to face trial. It makes sure that criminals can't avoid punishment just by crossing state lines.

What happened if an enslaved person escaped slavery and went to another state?

> *"No Person held to Service or Labour in one State, under the Laws thereof, escaping into another, shall, in Consequence of any Law or Regulation therein, be discharged from such Service or Labour, but shall be delivered up on Claim of the Party to whom such Service or Labour may be due."*

This rule was known as the Fugitive Slave Clause, and it

required that enslaved people who escaped to free states had to be returned to their enslavers. However, after the Thirteenth Amendment abolished slavery in 1865, this rule became invalid, meaning that it is no longer in effect today.

SECTION 3: NEW STATES & U.S. TERRITORIES

How do new states join the U.S.?

> *"New States may be admitted by the Congress into this Union..."*

Only Congress can approve new states joining the country. If a territory wants to become a state, Congress has to give its approval. This is how the U.S. grew from the original thirteen colonies to the fifty states we have today. Hawaii and Alaska were the last to join, becoming states in 1959.

Can states split up or merge into one?

> *"but no new State shall be formed or erected within the Jurisdiction of any other State; nor any State be formed by the Junction of two or more States, or Parts of States, without the Consent of the Legislatures of the States concerned as well as of the Congress."*

A new state can't be created by splitting up an existing state or merging states unless both Congress and the states involved agree. This rule was added to make sure states can't change their borders without proper agreement.

Although it's rare, this has happened before. Kentucky separated from Virginia in 1792, Maine split from Massachusetts in 1820, and West Virginia broke away from Virginia during the Civil War in 1863. However, no two states have ever merged into one.

Who is in charge of U.S. territories?

> *"The Congress shall have Power to dispose of and make all needful Rules and Regulations respecting the Territory or other Property belonging to the United States; and nothing in this Constitution shall be so construed as to Prejudice any Claims of the United States, or of any particular State."*

The Constitution gives Congress authority over U.S. territories, such as Puerto Rico, Guam, U.S. Virgin Islands, American Samoa, and the Northern Mariana Islands. Some have permanent residents with local governments, and most people there are U.S. citizens. Others have no permanent population and are mainly used for military, research, or conservation.

These territories are part of the U.S. but not states. Congress decides how they are governed and whether they might become states in the future. Some former territories, like Hawaii and Alaska, eventually became states, while others remain territories today, each with its own relationship with the U.S.

SECTION 4: THE FEDERAL GOVERNMENT'S PROMISES

What does the government have to do for each state?

> *"The United States shall guarantee to every State in this Union a Republican Form of Government, and shall protect each of them against Invasion; and on*

Application of the Legislature, or of the Executive (when the Legislature cannot be convened) against domestic Violence."

The federal government makes three big promises to each and every state:

1. This clause guarantees each state a "Republican Form of Government." This doesn't refer to the Republican Party we know today. Instead, it means every state must have a government where people elect their leaders (a republic)—not a system ruled by a king or dictator.
2. The federal government must protect states from invasion. If another country attacks a state, the U.S. military must step in to defend it.
3. The U.S. promises to help states stop major violence or uprisings. If a state is dealing with a rebellion, riot, or other crisis, the state's governor or legislature can ask the federal government for help. Today, this also includes sending help during natural disasters or other major emergencies to keep people safe.

ARTICLE V

How to Change the Constitution

Article V explains how the Constitution can be changed. Unlike the previous articles, it's just one short paragraph, but don't let that fool you—it does something truly unique. It tells us how to change the Constitution itself.

The framers knew that as the country grew, the Constitution would need to adapt too, so they created a way to add or update laws. But they didn't want it to be too easy.

Big changes to the nation's foundation should take serious thought and strong support, not happen on a whim. That's why the process of making changes, called amendments, is long and difficult. This ensures that only important and widely supported changes become the law of the land.

Since it was created, the Constitution has been amended twenty-seven times. These amendments address major issues like ending slavery, giving women the right to vote, and lowering the voting age to 18.

Each amendment brought a significant change, so even though amendments are rare, they've had a huge impact on shaping the country. (You'll learn more about each and every one of the twenty-seven amendments later in this book.)

Now, let's take a close look at how the framers designed a way to change the nation's highest law while still protecting its core principles.

How is a Constitutional amendment proposed?

> *"The Congress, whenever two thirds of both Houses shall deem it necessary, shall propose Amendments to this Constitution, or, on the Application of the Legislatures of two thirds of the several States, shall call a Convention for proposing Amendments..."*

The framers created two ways to propose an amendment to the Constitution:

1. Congress can propose an amendment if two-thirds of the House and Senate agree to it. This is how nearly all amendments in U.S. history have started.
2. Or, two-thirds of the states (today that's 34 states) can call for a special convention to propose an amendment. This method has never been used but it's there as a backup if enough states want to make a change.

How does an amendment actually get approved?

> *"which, in either Case, shall be valid to all Intents and Purposes, as Part of this Constitution, when ratified by the Legislatures of three fourths of the several States, or by Conventions in three fourths thereof, as the one or the other Mode of Ratification may be proposed by the Congress..."*

After an amendment is proposed, it needs to be approved by the states. Again, there are two ways this happens:

1. Three-fourths of state legislatures (today that's 38 states) must vote to approve it. This is the most common way amendments have been ratified.

2. Or, special conventions in three-fourths of the states (38 states) must approve it. This has only happened once—for the Twenty-First Amendment.

Why make it so hard to amend the Constitution and require 38 states to agree? The framers did this on purpose. They wanted to make sure that only the most important and widely-supported changes became law. By creating a challenging process, they ensured that amendments wouldn't happen too easily or too often, and that the Constitution would remain stable and balanced, while still allowing for necessary updates.

Are there limits to what can be amended?

> *"Provided that no Amendment which may be made prior to the Year One thousand eight hundred and eight shall in any Manner affect the first and fourth Clauses in the Ninth Section of the first Article..."*

When the Constitution was written, the framers temporarily protected certain parts from being changed. This rule prevented amendments from being made before 1808 that would affect the slave trade or direct taxes (like a tax on imported goods). This was a compromise made to appease Southern states that relied on slavery and trade.

After 1808, these restrictions expired, meaning amendments could be made to change those parts of the Constitution. Eventually, slavery was abolished in 1865 by the Thirteenth Amendment, and tax laws were changed in 1913 by the Sixteenth Amendment, which allowed Congress to create a federal income tax.

What can't be amended in the Constitution?

"and that no State, without its Consent, shall be deprived of its equal Suffrage in the Senate."

This line means that no amendment can be made that takes away a state's equal representation in the Senate without that state's permission. This rule was included to protect the balance of power between states, especially less-populated ones, so they have an equal say in the Senate.

ARTICLE VI

The Constitution is the Supreme Law

Article VI makes it crystal clear that the Constitution is the highest law in the United States, meaning that no other law—state or federal—can go against it. It covers three major points: honoring the country's old debts and agreements, making sure the Constitution is above all other laws, and requiring government officials to support it.

How did the Constitution handle past U.S. debts?

> *"All Debts contracted and Engagements entered into, before the Adoption of this Constitution, shall be as valid against the United States under this Constitution, as under the Confederation."*

When the Constitution was written, the United States owed money and had agreements with other countries from its earlier government system, the Articles of Confederation.

This part of Article VI says the U.S. would still keep those promises and pay its debts, even though the government had changed. In other words, the U.S. wasn't going to walk away from its debts or promises just because it had a new system of government.

Is there any law above the Constitution?

> *"This Constitution, and the Laws of the United States which shall be made in Pursuance thereof; and all Treaties made, or which shall be made, under the*

> *Authority of the United States, shall be the supreme Law of the Land..."*

This section makes it clear that the Constitution is the "supreme law of the land." It says that the Constitution, along with federal laws and treaties, is above any state laws. This is called the Supremacy Clause. It means that if a state law conflicts with federal law, the federal law always wins. This helps keep things consistent across all states and prevents states from passing laws that go against the Constitution.

Have you ever heard anyone say a law or court decision is "unconstitutional"? That means it goes against what the Constitution allows. For example, if a state tried to pass a law restricting free speech, it would be unconstitutional because the First Amendment protects that right. (You'll see more on that when we get to the First Amendment!)

Some cases of conflict between state and federal law are pretty straightforward, but many are not. Questions about whether something violates the Constitution can be complex and hotly-debated, even among experts. Sometimes, reasonable Constitutional scholars have different interpretations of the same issue. These disagreements are a major part of Constitutional law and are often settled by the courts, sometimes even reaching the Supreme Court for a final decision.

Do state courts also have to follow the Constitution?

> *"and the Judges in every State shall be bound thereby, any Thing in the Constitution or Laws of any State to the Contrary notwithstanding."*

Yes! This rule makes sure that state judges must follow the Constitution, even if their state's laws say something different. This means that when a state law conflicts with the Constitution, a state judge must follow the Constitution instead. It ensures that all courts in the country—state or federal—respect the highest law of the land.

Who has to take an oath to support the Constitution?

> *"The Senators and Representatives before mentioned, and the Members of the several State Legislatures, and all executive and judicial Officers, both of the United States and of the several States, shall be bound by Oath or Affirmation, to support this Constitution..."*

Everyone who holds a government job in the United States—whether at the federal, state, or local level—must take an oath to support the Constitution. This includes all members of Congress, state lawmakers, judges, governors, the President, and other executive officers. Even people who work in the government but aren't elected, like law enforcement officers, take an oath to uphold the Constitution.

This oath means they're promising to follow the Constitution and its rules, no matter what their personal beliefs might be. It's a reminder that the Constitution is the ultimate set of rules for everyone in government and that all officials, no matter their role, are expected to respect and protect it.

Can people of any religion get government jobs?

> *"but no religious Test shall ever be required as a Qualification to any Office or public Trust under the United States."*

The Constitution clearly states that there can't be any kind of religious requirement to hold a government job. This means people of all religions—or no religion at all—can work in government. Today, this might seem obvious, but it's a powerful example of how the Constitution shaped American society. The framers wanted to make sure that the government stayed fair and open to everyone, no matter their beliefs, and that no one would be excluded or treated unfairly because of their religion. At the time, this was a big change from many other countries, where religion and government were closely tied. Now, this freedom is a core part of how Americans think about government and fairness.

ARTICLE VII

How the Constitution Was Approved

Article VII is the final article of the original Constitution. It's short but powerful—a simple statement that explains how the Constitution became the official law of the United States. This article lays out what needed to happen for the Constitution to be ratified by the original states, turning it from an idea into the foundation of American government.

What was the approval process for the Constitution?

> *"The Ratification of the Conventions of nine States, shall be sufficient for the Establishment of this Constitution between the States so ratifying the Same."*

The framers decided that the Constitution would go into effect once nine out of the original thirteen states agreed to it. This was a big deal because it showed that the framers wanted strong support before the Constitution could become law. They could have required all thirteen states to approve it, but setting the requirement at nine made it more likely to happen, while still showing that most states supported the new government.

When did the framers finish the Constitution?

> *"done in Convention by the Unanimous Consent of the States present the Seventeenth Day of September in the Year of our Lord one thousand seven hundred and Eighty seven..."*

After all the debating and hard work, thirty-nine delegates—representatives chosen to speak and decide on behalf of their states—signed the Constitution in Philadelphia on September 17, 1787.

These weren't just politicians; they were people from different states, backgrounds, and perspectives, all coming together to shape the future of the United States. Some names, like George Washington and Benjamin Franklin, will sound familiar. But many of the signers were everyday people who believed in the promise of this new government, even if they aren't household names today.

Who signed the Constitution?

At the bottom of the Constitution, you'll find the signatures of the thirty-nine delegates who helped draft it.

The first name listed is George Washington, who presided over the Constitutional Convention. His signature, along with those of the other delegates, represented their agreement to the final document.

The signers came from twelve of the thirteen original states: Connecticut, Delaware, Georgia, Maryland, Massachusetts, New Hampshire, New Jersey, New York, North Carolina, Pennsylvania, South Carolina, and Virginia. Rhode Island refused to send delegates and did not take part.

Some of the most well-known signers include James Madison, often called the "Father of the Constitution," Alexander Hamilton, who strongly advocated for a powerful federal government, and Benjamin Franklin, the oldest delegate at the convention.

Not every founding father signed the Constitution. Some, like Thomas Jefferson and John Adams, were serving as diplomats overseas. Others, like Patrick Henry, refused to support it, believing it gave the federal government too much power.

The long list of signatures is a reminder that this historic document was a team effort. It wasn't just the vision of one or two leaders; it was a massive collaborative project—a "group chat" of the eighteenth century—with each person bringing their own ideas and values to create something that would last for generations.

When did the Constitution get approved?

Although the Constitution was signed by the framers in 1787, that didn't mean it was officially in effect. Each state needed to hold a convention where representatives of the people debated and voted on whether to accept it. The Constitution officially became the law of the land on June 21, 1788, when New Hampshire became the ninth state to ratify it.

The first nine states to approve the Constitution, in the order they ratified it, were Delaware, Pennsylvania, New Jersey, Georgia, Connecticut, Massachusetts, Maryland, South Carolina, and finally New Hampshire. Once these nine had ratified, the Constitution was officially adopted.

Did all thirteen original states eventually ratify it?

Yes, eventually all thirteen original states approved the Constitution, though it took time. After New Hampshire's ratification made it official, the remaining four states joined gradually: Virginia, New York, North Carolina, and finally Rhode Island. Rhode Island held out the longest, not ratifying until May 29, 1790—by which time the new government was already up and running.

Wait, the Constitution has typos?

> *"The Word, "the," being interlined between the seventh and eighth Lines of the first Page, The Word "Thirty" being partly written on an Erazure in the fifteenth Line of the first Page, The Words "is tried" being interlined between the thirty second and thirty third Lines of the first Page and the Word "the" being interlined between the forty third and forty fourth Lines of the second Page."*

Imagine finishing a huge project, only to realize you left out a word—but there's no delete key, no undo. That's essentially what happened with the Constitution. At the end of Article VII, there are handwritten corrections where the framers listed missing words and fixed small errors in spelling and formatting. These last-minute edits didn't change the meaning of the document, but they prove that even the most important papers in U.S. history needed a little proofreading. No autocorrect—just ink, patience, and probably a lot of frustration.

A Quick Note on Formatting

The way we go through the Amendments will look a little different from how we covered the Constitution's Articles. Since many Amendments are shorter, we'll start by reading each Amendment in full, then break it down point by point to explain what it means and how it affects you today. This will help make sure you understand both the big picture and the important details.

Imagine if the U.S. government could ban your favorite music, force you to follow a certain religion, or punish you for criticizing the President. Sounds extreme, right?

The Bill of Rights was created to prevent that—to make sure every person has rights that can't just be taken away.

When the Constitution was written in 1787, many people worried that it didn't do enough to protect individual rights. They didn't want a government that could silence them, invade their privacy, or imprison them unfairly. In fact, the Constitution might never have been ratified if the framers hadn't promised to add a Bill of Rights to address these concerns.

So, not long after the Constitution was signed, the First Congress proposed twelve amendments—known as the Joint Resolution of 1789—to lock in basic freedoms and limit government power. By 1791, ten of those twelve amendments were ratified and became what we now call the Bill of Rights.

This document gave people more confidence in the new government and protected many of the rights you might take for granted today, like free speech, religious freedom, fair trials, and protection from unreasonable searches.

But those weren't the only amendments ever added to the Constitution. Over time, more amendments were proposed and ratified to expand rights and fix important issues.

We'll get to those in the next section, but for now, let's focus on the first ten—the Bill of Rights—that form the foundation of American freedoms.

Here's something wild: one of the original twelve amendments that didn't make it into the Bill of Rights took over 200 years to get ratified, finally becoming the Twenty-Seventh Amendment in 1992. And the last one? Still unratified today. That's right—the Bill of Rights is part of an ongoing conversation about freedom and justice.

When people call the Constitution a "living document," this is exactly what they mean. It wasn't meant to stay frozen in time—it was designed to grow and change as the country evolved. The Bill of Rights, along with every amendment that came after it, proves that the fight for freedom, fairness, and justice is never really over. It's something every generation helps shape.

In this section, we're diving in deep because these rights are so important to you and your daily life. Some answers will be long and detailed, but that's because truly understanding them will make you the most informed citizen you can be. The better you know your rights, the better you can protect them—and maybe even help shape the future of freedom in America.

Let's get started.

AMENDMENT I

Your Basic Freedoms

The First Amendment is one of the most important parts of the Constitution because it protects many of the freedoms Americans value most: freedom of speech, religion, press, and protest.

These rights are at the heart of democracy, allowing people to express beliefs, share ideas, gather together, and push for change without fear of punishment. Without the rights guaranteed in the First Amendment, the government could control what people say, how they worship, or whether they can challenge those in power.

Let's explore these freedoms and how they are protected in the First Amendment.

> *"Congress shall make no law respecting an establishment of religion, or prohibiting the free exercise thereof; or abridging the freedom of speech, or of the press; or the right of the people peaceably to assemble, and to petition the Government for a redress of grievances."*

FREEDOM OF RELIGION

Can the government make me follow a certain religion?

> *"Congress shall make no law respecting an establishment of religion, or prohibiting the free exercise thereof..."*

Nope. The First Amendment ensures that in the U.S., you are free to practice any religion—or no religion at all. This means that Congress can't pass laws that establish a national religion, favor one faith over another, or punish people for their religious beliefs (or lack of them).

When the Constitution was written, this idea was radical. Many countries had official state religions, and people could be punished for practicing the "wrong" faith. The framers wanted to avoid that by making sure that religion remains a personal choice, not a government decision.

The First Amendment protects personal beliefs while ensuring no one is forced to follow religious rules they don't believe in. It guarantees that you get to decide what you believe—not the government.

However, freedom of religion doesn't mean people can do anything they want in the name of faith. Religious beliefs don't override all laws.

For example, someone can't commit a crime and claim it's legal because of their religion. If a religious practice causes harm, the government can step in to stop it, even if that religion allows it. Businesses also can't discriminate against people purely based on religion, unless there is a specific legal exemption.

Balancing religious freedom with other rights and laws can be complicated. Sometimes, one law has to take priority over another. This is why courts often have to step in and decide where the limits are—ensuring that freedom of religion is protected while also keeping things fair for everyone.

FREEDOM OF SPEECH

Do I have the right to say whatever I want?

> *"Congress shall make no law...abridging the freedom of speech..."*

Yes, but with some limits. The First Amendment protects freedom of speech, meaning you have the right to express your thoughts, opinions, and beliefs without the government stopping you. The key word in this excerpt, "abridging," means to limit or restrict. So when the First Amendment says Congress can't abridge freedom of speech, it means the government can't make laws that unfairly restrict what people are allowed to say.

Think about it like this: If you post something on social media—whether it's your thoughts on climate change, criticism of a government policy, or even a meme making fun of a public figure—freedom of speech means the government can't punish you for it.

This protection is a huge part of our democracy, allowing people to question authority, debate ideas, and push for change without fear of arrest or punishment.

But free speech doesn't mean you can say absolutely anything without consequences. Some types of speech are not protected by the Constitution because they cause harm. For example, making violent threats, encouraging illegal activity, or spreading false information that causes panic (like yelling "fire" in a crowded theater when there isn't one) aren't covered by the First Amendment.

That said, most opinions and ideas—even ones that are controversial or unpopular—are protected. Whether you're speaking out about social issues, joining a protest, or creating art that challenges authority, the First Amendment ensures that your voice can be part of the conversation.

FREEDOM OF THE PRESS

Can the government control what the media says?

> *"Congress shall make no law...abridging the freedom... of the press..."*

No, the U.S. government can't control, censor, or shut down news outlets just because it doesn't like what they're reporting. The First Amendment protects freedom of the press, meaning that newspapers, TV news, radio, websites, podcasts, and other media can publish information and opinions without government interference. You'll notice the word "abridging" again here, just like in freedom of speech—and you'll see it a few more times as we go through the First Amendment. It's a reminder that the government isn't allowed to restrict or control fundamental rights.

This protection is a huge deal because an independent press keeps the public informed, especially about what government leaders are doing. In many other countries—even today—governments limit what the media can report, or even shut down news outlets that criticize them. In the U.S., however, the First Amendment ensures that journalists can investigate, question, and report on important issues without fear of being silenced or punished.

A free press is crucial in a democracy. It holds leaders accountable, exposes corruption, and helps citizens stay informed. Freedom of the press isn't just about letting journalists do their jobs—it's about making sure everyone has access to the truth, even when that truth is inconvenient for people in power.

FREEDOM OF ASSEMBLY

Can the government stop people protesting peacefully?

> *"Congress shall make no law...abridging...the right of the people peaceably to assemble..."*

Nope. The U.S. government can't stop people from gathering peacefully to protest, march, or rally for a cause even if it's against the government itself. This right, called freedom of assembly, allows people to "assemble" in groups, express their opinions, and demand change—as long as it's done without violence.

For example, if you and thousands of others want to join a climate change march, attend a racial justice protest, or participate in a rally for mental health awareness, this freedom of assembly protects your right to do so peacefully. Even if the government disagrees with what you're protesting, they can't shut it down just because they don't like it. Freedom of assembly is a powerful tool for change, letting Americans come together to make sure they're heard, no matter who or what they're protesting.

But freedom of assembly doesn't mean people can do whatever they want during a protest. Protests must be peaceful. Violent riots, destruction of property, and harm to others aren't protected under the Constitution. The government can also set reasonable rules for things like where and when large gatherings happen (for example, requiring permits for protests in major public spaces).

RIGHT TO PETITION

Can I ask the government to change things I don't like?

> *"Congress shall make no law...abridging...the right...to petition the Government for a redress of grievances."*

Yes! The First Amendment protects the right to petition the government, meaning that if a law, policy, or government action seems unfair, harmful, or just plain wrong, people have the power to challenge it and demand change. This right ensures that everyone—no matter their age, background, or beliefs—has a way to be heard by those in power.

This is not the same as freedom of assembly. It's listed separately because the right to petition isn't just about gathering in public and speaking out—it also includes direct action to push for change. People can write letters to their representatives, gather signatures on petitions, lobby lawmakers, and even take the government to court if they believe their rights have been violated.

For example, if you want stronger environmental protections, you could start a petition asking lawmakers to pass stricter pollution laws. If a city government tries to ban peaceful protests in public spaces, people could write letters to local officials and rally community support to challenge the decision. And if a state passes a voting law that makes it harder for certain groups to vote, civil rights organizations could sue the government, arguing that the law violates the Constitution.

The right to petition is like a direct line to the people in power, giving citizens the ability to push for positive change in their communities, their states, and the entire country.

AMENDMENT II

The Right to Keep and Bear Arms

The Second Amendment is one of the most debated parts of the U.S. Constitution. It's only one sentence long, but it has sparked centuries of discussion about gun rights, public safety, self-defense, and government regulation. This amendment affects laws in your community, school policies, and national debates that might directly impact your life, making it an important topic to understand.

Let's start by reading the exact wording of the amendment, then break down what it actually means and why it matters today.

> *"A well regulated Militia, being necessary to the security of a free State, the right of the people to keep and bear Arms, shall not be infringed."*

Wait...what does that actually mean?

This one sentence has led to a lot of debate, but the overall idea is that since security is necessary for a free country, people have the right to own and carry weapons, and the government can't take that right away.

That sounds simple, but it leaves many questions open to interpretation. What counts as "security"? What kind of weapons ("arms") does this cover? Who exactly has this right? These questions are still debated today, and courts continue to decide how the Second Amendment applies in modern times.

Why is the Second Amendment controversial?

The phrase "keep and bear arms" is short, but it has been interpreted in many different ways. In general, people agree that it means citizens have the right to own and carry weapons. But, like many parts of the Constitution, people interpret *exactly* what this means in many different ways. That's why there's so much debate.

One thing most people do agree on is that the Second Amendment doesn't mean anyone can own any weapon they want, whenever and wherever they want. Federal and state laws set rules on who can own guns, what kinds are allowed, and where they can be carried. But the exact meaning of the Second Amendment is still argued in courts and the media. Some states have stricter gun laws than others, and some legal cases even go to the Supreme Court to determine what the Second Amendment allows.

Because there's so much discussion around it, the Second Amendment often comes up in conversations about gun safety, school safety, self-defense, public policy, and personal rights. It plays a major role in laws about who can own guns, where they can carry them, and what limits should exist for public safety. People—including courts, lawmakers, and communities—are still debating what it really means, and new laws continue to shape how it applies today.

People often have strong opinions about the best way to keep everyone safe. So whether you're talking with friends, seeing news about gun laws, or thinking about the rules in your own community, understanding the history behind this amendment will help you join the conversation and form your own opinions.

What is a "well regulated militia"?

We've seen the term "militia" before in Article I, Section 8 of the Constitution, where Congress was given the power to call on militias for defense. The idea was that each community would have a "well-regulated militia," meaning a group that was organized, trained, and ready to help keep the country safe. Back then, these militias were considered an essential part of national security. Today, however, the U.S. has a standing military and organized police forces, so most people don't think about militias the same way.

Can anyone own a gun under the Second Amendment?

While the Second Amendment protects the right to own and carry firearms, it has limits. Over time, federal and state laws have been passed about who can own guns, what kinds are allowed, and where they can be carried. Here are some examples:

- **Background checks:** When someone wants to buy a gun, they usually have to pass a background check. This ensures they meet legal requirements for owning a gun and don't have a criminal record or history of violence that would make them ineligible.
- **Age restrictions:** Federal law sets minimum age requirements for purchasing firearms, though states may have stricter rules. These age limits are meant to ensure that people are mature enough to handle guns responsibly.
- **Weapon-free zones:** Schools, government buildings, and other public places often ban weapons to create safe environments. For example, most schools do not allow weapons on campus, even if someone has the legal right to carry them elsewhere.

AMENDMENT III

Ban on Forced Housing of Troops

The Third Amendment is one of the least discussed parts of the Bill of Rights, but it was a big deal when it was written. It was created in response to a real problem that American colonists faced under British rule: being forced to let soldiers live in their homes. While this might not seem like a major issue today, the amendment represents a key idea that *is* still relevant to your life: the government can't use your personal property without your permission.

Let's read the exact wording of the Third Amendment, then break down what it means and the parts that still matter today.

> *"No Soldier shall, in time of peace be quartered in any house, without the consent of the Owner, nor in time of war, but in a manner to be prescribed by law."*

What does this actually say?

The government can't force people to let soldiers stay in their homes during peacetime—it can only happen if the homeowner agrees. Even in wartime, soldiers can't be housed in private homes unless Congress passes specific laws allowing it.

Why was this amendment created?

Before the American Revolution, the British government passed laws called the Quartering Acts, which forced

American colonists to let British soldiers stay in their homes. People had no choice—they had to give up space, food, and supplies to soldiers without any payment. Many saw this as a serious invasion of privacy and personal property.

After gaining independence from Britain, the framers wanted to make sure this never happened again. They believed that people's homes should be protected from government overreach—a value that still matters today.

Does the Third Amendment matter today?

At first glance, the Third Amendment might seem outdated since the government doesn't force people to house soldiers anymore. However, it still represents an important principle: protecting personal privacy and property from government intrusion.

Some legal scholars argue that this amendment indirectly supports the right to privacy, which has been used in cases about government surveillance, property rights, and personal freedoms. While the Third Amendment isn't often debated in modern court cases, it helps set the foundation for the idea that the government can't enter your home or personal space without permission.

Today, while it's unlikely you'll ever be asked to house a soldier, the Third Amendment is still important because it reinforces the idea that your home is your own private space—and the government can't invade it without a really good reason.

AMENDMENT IV

Protection from Unreasonable Searches and Seizures

The Fourth Amendment is also about privacy and protecting people from government overreach. It promises that law enforcement can't search you, your home, your belongings, or take your property without a good reason. This amendment is one of the most important legal protections in everyday life because it affects how police and the government can investigate crimes, gather evidence, and enforce laws.

Read the exact wording, then discover how it applies to real-life situations today:

> *"The right of the people to be secure in their persons, houses, papers, and effects, against unreasonable searches and seizures, shall not be violated, and no Warrants shall issue, but upon probable cause, supported by Oath or affirmation, and particularly describing the place to be searched, and the persons or things to be seized."*

Can police search my home without my permission?

No, not without a good reason. The Fourth Amendment says people have the right to be secure in their houses, papers, and belongings. In this context, "papers" refers to personal documents, like letters, records, journals, or other private information. Today, this means more than physical papers and includes things like emails, text messages, and digital files. This means the police can't just walk into your house and search it—or go through your computer—without a valid reason.

However, there are exceptions. If the police see something illegal in plain sight, meaning they can clearly see evidence of a crime without searching for it (like a stolen item sitting on a table near an open door), they may not need a warrant.

Also, if there's an urgent reason, such as believing someone inside is in danger or a crime is actively happening, they can enter without a warrant under what's called "exigent circumstances."

But in most cases, if the police don't have a warrant, you don't have to let them in.

Do the police need a warrant to go through my phone?

Most of the time, no. Police typically need a warrant to search your phone. Since texts, emails, photos, search history, and location data contain personal and private details, the Supreme Court ruled in *Riley v. California* (2014) that warrants are required in most situations—just like with home searches.

However, there are exceptions. If you give police permission to search your phone (or home, computer, etc.), a warrant isn't needed. In some cases, if a person is arrested, police may be allowed to search certain parts of their phone, depending on the situation. Additionally, in "exigent circumstances"—such as an immediate threat to safety or the risk of evidence being destroyed—police may be allowed to conduct a search without a warrant.

Because technology is constantly evolving, many cases about privacy rights, phone searches, and online data collection end up in the Supreme Court.

What about track my phone? Or read my social media?

This is one of the biggest modern debates around the Fourth Amendment. When the Constitution was written, the framers couldn't have imagined cell phones, GPS, and social media, so courts are still working out how digital privacy rights apply today.

In general, law enforcement needs a warrant to track your phone, read private messages, or collect large amounts of data about you. However, some government agencies can collect certain data without a warrant, especially if it's publicly available, like social media posts, public wifi check-ins, or location data from certain apps.

In an age where technology makes it easier than ever to track people, monitor activity, and collect personal data, the Fourth Amendment is more important than ever.

Courts will continue to decide how it applies to new issues, but the fundamental idea remains the same: your privacy matters, and the government can't take it away without a valid reason.

Remember, laws can also vary depending on where you live, and they may change over time. So while this information is based on established legal rules, it's always a good idea to stay updated on any changes. If you're ever unsure about your rights, looking up reliable legal resources or speaking with a lawyer can help.

What is "probable cause"? When do police need it?

The Fourth Amendment protects against unreasonable searches and seizures, but it doesn't stop police from searching when they have a legitimate reason. The next part explains what's required for a legal search:

> "... and no Warrants shall issue, but upon probable cause, supported by Oath or affirmation, and particularly describing the place to be searched, and the persons or things to be seized."

"Probable cause" means police need real evidence or a strong reason to believe a crime is happening before they can get a warrant or search without one.

A judge has to approve a warrant, and it must specifically describe what place is being searched and what the police are looking for. This prevents random searches and ensures police can't just go through everything you own without a reason.

If I get pulled over, can the police search my car?

It depends. Cars are treated differently than houses under the Fourth Amendment because they are mobile, meaning evidence inside could be moved or destroyed before a warrant can be obtained.

If an officer has probable cause, they can search your car without a warrant. For example, if they see illegal items in plain view, smell something suspicious, or believe the car is involved in a crime, they may be able to search it on the spot.

What if police search something illegal?

If police violate the Fourth Amendment by conducting an illegal search or seizure, any evidence they find can't be used in court. This is called the exclusionary rule, which means that if officers break the law to obtain evidence, it can't be used against someone in a trial. The idea behind this rule is to prevent law enforcement from ignoring Constitutional rights just to make arrests.

Can my school search my backpack or locker?

Schools follow different rules than police. Students do have Fourth Amendment rights at school, but because schools are responsible for student safety, they don't always need probable cause or a warrant to conduct a search like the police do. A school official can search a backpack, locker, or personal items if they have reasonable suspicion—which is a lower standard than probable cause. This means they need a solid reason to believe you may have something illegal or dangerous but don't need the same level of proof as the police do.

AMENDMENT V

The Right to Due Process and Protection from Self-Incrimination

The Fifth Amendment is one of the strongest protections against government abuse. It ensures that people get fair trials, don't have to testify against themselves, and can't be punished unfairly. It also protects personal property from being taken without fair payment. You've probably heard of "pleading the Fifth"—that comes from this amendment! But it covers much more than the right to remain silent.

Can I be charged with a serious crime without proof?

> *"No person shall be held to answer for a capital, or otherwise infamous crime, unless on a presentment or indictment of a Grand Jury..."*

This rule exists to prevent wrongful accusations by making sure the government can't put someone on trial for a serious crime without first proving there's enough evidence.

A "grand jury" is a group of regular citizens who decide whether there is enough evidence for someone to be formally charged with a serious crime. Instead of a prosecutor alone deciding to press charges, a grand jury adds an extra layer of protection, requiring the government to prove there's a strong case before moving forward. This process is meant to protect people from unfair prosecutions, making sure that serious criminal charges aren't based on weak or unproven claims.

This rule applies to "capital" crimes, meaning crimes that could result in the death penalty, and other serious offenses ("infamous crimes"). However, not all criminal cases require a grand jury. For less serious crimes, prosecutors can file charges without one.

Are there grand juries in military trials?

> *"except in cases arising in the land or naval forces, or in the Militia, when in actual service in time of War or public danger..."*

No. The Fifth Amendment's grand jury requirement does not apply to members of the military who are on active duty during war or national emergencies. Instead, military members are subject to a different legal system called military law, which has its own rules for trials and punishments.

Can I be tried for the same crime over and over?

> *"nor shall any person be subject for the same offence to be twice put in jeopardy of life or limb..."*

No. If you're found not guilty of a crime, the government can't put you on trial again for that exact crime, even if new evidence is found later. This protection is called "double jeopardy", meaning your life and freedom can't be put in "jeopardy" (danger) twice for the same crime. It prevents unfair retrials, protects people from being harassed by the legal system, and makes sure the government only gets one fair chance to prove its case. The government also can't appeal a verdict of not guilty, so once that happens, the case is closed.

Double jeopardy only applies when a person is found not guilty. If someone is found guilty (convicted), they can appeal the decision to a higher court, asking for the ruling against them to be overturned.

An appeal is not the same as being tried twice—it's a request to review the first trial for mistakes, like unfair legal procedures. If the appeal is successful, the case may be retried, but that's because the original trial was found to be flawed, not because the government is trying to convict the person again unfairly.

Appeals protect defendants by making sure trials are fair, while double jeopardy stops the government from repeatedly prosecuting someone for the same crime.

What does "pleading the Fifth" mean?

> *"No person shall...be compelled in any criminal case to be a witness against himself..."*

If you've ever seen a TV show where someone refuses to answer questions in court by saying, "I plead the Fifth," they're using their Fifth Amendment right against self-incrimination. This means you can't be forced to confess to a crime or say anything that might be used against you in court. In other words, you can't be forced to be "a witness against yourself."

As you've probably also heard in TV shows, you have the right to remain silent when being questioned by the police. But this right also applies in a trial—you can plead the Fifth to refuse to answer questions that could make you look guilty.

What is "due process"?

> *"No person shall...be deprived of life, liberty, or property, without due process of law..."*

"Due process" means the government has to follow fair procedures before punishing someone. They can't just throw someone in jail, take away their rights, or seize their property without following legal steps. This is a very important protection that ensures everyone is treated fairly under the law, giving people a chance to defend themselves in court before the government can take action against them. It prevents unfair arrests, wrongful convictions, and government abuse of power.

Can the government take my property?

> *"Nor shall private property be taken for public use, without just compensation."*

Yes, but they have to pay you for it. This part of the Fifth Amendment protects people from the government taking their property without fair payment. If the government needs a piece of private property—like land—to build a highway, school, or public project, they must pay the owner a fair price.

This is called eminent domain—the government can take land, but they can't do it for free. While this power is legal, it's often controversial, especially if people don't want to sell their property or they feel the payment isn't fair.

AMENDMENT VI

The Right to a Fair Trial

The Sixth Amendment protects your rights if you're accused of a crime. It guarantees you a fair and speedy trial. It also gives you the right to know your charges, have an "impartial" (unbiased) jury, a lawyer, and witnesses to defend you. Without these rights, people could be imprisoned without knowing their charges, face biased juries, or be convicted without being able to defend themselves. In short, this amendment protects one of the most important rights in the justice system: the right to defend yourself.

How fast does a trial have to happen?

> *"In all criminal prosecutions, the accused shall enjoy the right to a speedy and public trial..."*

If you're accused of a crime, the government can't leave you sitting in jail forever, waiting for a trial. You have the right to a "speedy" trial, which means it must happen within a reasonable time so you don't lose months or years of your life waiting for justice.

For example, if someone was arrested but had to wait years for a trial, they could lose their job, home, or relationships before even getting a chance to prove their innocence. The Sixth Amendment prevents that from happening.

This rule also says that trials have to be public, meaning they can't be done in secret, which helps prevent unfair treatment and corruption.

Where are juries selected from for a trial?

> *"by an impartial jury of the State and district wherein the crime shall have been committed, which district shall have been previously ascertained by law…"*

If you're on trial, your jury must come from the same state and district where the crime happened. This rule ensures that your case is decided by people from your own community, not by strangers from another part of the country who might not understand the local circumstances.

Imagine being arrested in your hometown but judged by a jury from a completely different region. They might have a very different perspective on laws or local issues. To prevent that, this Amendment guarantees that trials take place where the crime occurred, with a local and neutral jury.

Do I have the right to know what I'm being accused of?

> *"and to be informed of the nature and cause of the accusation…"*

Yes! The government can't charge you with a crime and keep the details a secret. If you're accused, you have the right to know exactly what you're being charged with so you can prepare a defense. Imagine getting arrested and thrown in jail but no one tells you what you did wrong. You'd have no way to defend yourself. This part of the amendment prevents that.

Can I question people who testify against me?

> *"to be confronted with the witnesses against him…"*

Yes. If someone testifies against you, you or your lawyer have the right to face them in court and question them. This prevents the government from using secret witnesses or anonymous accusations to convict people unfairly. For example, if someone accused you of stealing, they would have to stand in court and answer questions from your lawyer.

Can I bring my own witnesses to defend me in court?

> *"to have compulsory process for obtaining witnesses in his favor…"*

Absolutely! If you're on trial, you can bring witnesses who can help prove your innocence. The court must allow them to testify and can't stop people from coming forward to defend you. For example, if you were accused of a crime but a friend saw you somewhere else at the time it happened, they have the right to testify in your defense. This ensures you have a fair chance to prove the truth.

Can I always have a lawyer? What if I can't afford one?

> *"and to have the Assistance of Counsel for his defence."*

Yes! If you're charged with a crime, you always have the right to a lawyer. If you can't afford one, the government must provide one to you for free—this is called a public defender. Having a lawyer is crucial because the legal system is complicated, and trying to defend yourself without one can hurt your case. A lawyer knows how to challenge evidence, question witnesses, and make sure your rights are protected. The Sixth Amendment ensures that everyone—no matter their financial situation—gets legal representation so that no one is left to face the justice system alone.

AMENDMENT VII

The Right to a Jury in Civil Cases

While the Sixth Amendment protects jury trials in *criminal* cases, the Seventh Amendment ensures the same right applies to certain *civil* (non-criminal) disputes. It also ensures that judges can't unfairly overrule a jury's decision.

What is a "civil case"?

A civil case is a legal dispute between people, businesses, or organizations, rather than a case about a crime. Civil cases often involve money, contracts, property, or personal injuries. Unlike criminal trials—where the government is trying to punish someone for breaking the law—civil trials are about solving disagreements and determining responsibility.

Some examples of civil cases are:

- a music artist suing a company for using their song without permission (copyright case)
- a person suing a store after slipping and getting injured because the floor was wet and there were no warning signs (personal injury case)
- a dispute between a landlord and tenant over unpaid rent (contract dispute case),
- a customer taking a brand to court over a defective product that caused harm (product liability case)

In these situations, the jury listens to the evidence and decides if one side should pay money to the other.

Do I have the right to a jury in every type of lawsuit?

"In Suits at common law, where the value in controversy shall exceed twenty dollars, the right of trial by jury shall be preserved..."

Not always. The Seventh Amendment gives people the right to a jury trial in civil cases, but only when the case involves a significant amount of money. When this amendment was written, the twenty dollars mentioned was a large amount, but today, courts set the minimum much higher. The exact amount can vary by state, as there is no nationwide minimum.

For example, if you sue someone for damages in a personal injury case or a business dispute, you might have the right to a jury. But for cases called "small claims" (like suing a neighbor for a minor issue), courts often don't require a jury. Instead, a judge will decide the case.

Can a judge overrule a jury's decision in a civil case?

"and no fact tried by a jury, shall be otherwise re-examined in any Court of the United States, than according to the rules of the common law."

In most cases, no. If a jury makes a decision in a civil case, a judge can't just ignore it or overturn it because they disagree. The only way a jury's decision can be re-examined is through the appeal process, where a higher court reviews the case. This ensures that jury decisions are respected and that one person (the judge) doesn't have all the power in civil trials.

AMENDMENT VIII

Protection from Cruel and Unusual Punishment

The Eighth Amendment protects people from extreme punishments and unfair treatment in the justice system. It makes sure that bail and fines aren't unreasonably high and that people aren't punished in ways that are cruel or inhumane. The language of this Amendment is pretty simple and straightforward, so let's read the whole thing first:

> *"Excessive bail shall not be required, nor excessive fines imposed, nor cruel and unusual punishments inflicted."*

Can a court set bail at any amount they want?

No. If someone is arrested, the court can require them to pay bail—money that the accused person pays to be released from jail while waiting for trial. But the government can't ask for "excessive bail," meaning an unreasonably high amount, just to keep someone locked up unfairly.

For example, if someone is arrested for a minor offense, like shoplifting a candy bar, the court can't punish them by setting a $100,000 bail just to make sure they can't afford it and are forced to stay in jail until trial. The bail amount must be reasonable and based on the seriousness of the crime. However, judges can deny bail altogether in certain cases—meaning the accused person doesn't get an option to pay for release and must remain in jail until trial—such as when they are considered dangerous or a "flight risk" (meaning they are likely to run away and avoid trial).

Is a court allowed to give out huge fines for small crimes?

No. The government can't issue "excessive fines" that are way out of proportion to the crime. Fines are supposed to be a reasonable punishment, not a way to unfairly take money from people. For example, if someone forgets to pay for a bus ticket, the court can't fine them thousands of dollars. The fine has to match the severity of the offense, ensuring that small mistakes don't lead to extreme financial penalties..

What counts as "cruel and unusual punishment"?

The framers wanted to make sure the government can't punish people in ways that are extreme, inhumane, or out of proportion to the crime. This means no torture, extreme physical harm, or degrading treatment. By banning "cruel and unusual punishments," they meant that punishments must be fair and reasonable for the crime committed *and* must respect human dignity. For example, if someone is convicted of stealing a loaf of bread, the court can't sentence them to life in prison or a public beating.

AMENDMENT IX

Rights Beyond the Constitution

The framers knew they couldn't list every single right people have—or could have in the future—so the Ninth Amendment protects those unlisted rights from being ignored or taken away. It reminds us that the Constitution protects more than what's written on paper.

Does the Constitution cover *all* my rights?

> *"The enumeration in the Constitution, of certain rights, shall not be construed to deny or disparage others retained by the people."*

Nope! The Ninth Amendment makes it clear that the rights listed in the Constitution aren't the only rights you have.

The framers couldn't predict the future, so they left room for new rights to be recognized over time. The phrase "deny or disparage" means that just because a right isn't written down doesn't mean the government can ignore it or take it away, ensuring that unlisted rights still exist and deserve protection.

For example, the Constitution doesn't specifically say you have a right to privacy, but courts have ruled that privacy is a basic right protected under the Ninth Amendment. This has been used to protect your right to make choices about your own body, your freedom to travel between states without needing permission, and your right to keep your medical records private.

AMENDMENT X

States' Rights and Limits of Federal Power

The Tenth Amendment explains why laws can be different from state to state. It says that if the Constitution doesn't give a power to the federal government, that power belongs to the states or the people. The framers wanted to prevent the federal government from controlling everything, so they left many decisions to individual states and citizens. This amendment plays a key role in debates over whether the federal government can set national rules on issues like healthcare, drug legalization, and voting laws.

Why do some states have different laws than others?

> *"The powers not delegated to the United States by the Constitution, nor prohibited by it to the States, are reserved to the States respectively..."*

The framers wanted to make sure the federal government didn't get too powerful, so the Tenth Amendment gives states control over many areas of law, like education, state police forces, and local elections.

For example, the federal government can declare war, print money, and regulate immigration—because those powers are specifically listed in the Constitution. But things like setting driving laws, running public schools, and handling state taxes are state responsibilities, since the Constitution doesn't mention them. That's why driver's licenses are issued by states, not the federal government, and why driving laws—like speed limits or learner's permit ages—can vary between California, Texas, and New York. Similarly, each state can structure its own education system and tax rates, leading to differences across the country.

What about rights not controlled by the government?

> *"...or to the people."*

This recognizes that some rights and freedoms belong to individuals, not the government. The Tenth Amendment doesn't just protect state power—it also limits government control overall. For example, choosing your job, traveling freely between states, and making decisions about raising your kids are personal rights that the government can't take away. This amendment ensures that the government doesn't interfere too much in people's daily lives, keeping certain freedoms in the hands of individuals.

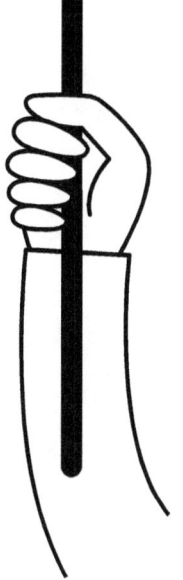

Changing the Constitution

Now we're moving on to the rest of the amendments—the ones added after the Bill of Rights. Unlike the first ten, which were passed all at once, these seventeen amendments were added one by one over more than 200 years to keep up with a changing country.

Some of them tweak how the government works, like setting rules for elections, presidential terms, and how officials are chosen. Others focus on civil rights, expanding freedoms—like ending slavery, giving women the right to vote, and granting citizenship to everyone born in the U.S., regardless of race. Some even deal with unexpected issues, like banning alcohol—and then bringing it back!

Unlike the Bill of Rights, which added protections to the Constitution, these later amendments do more than just add—they change, update, or even cancel out older rules.

For example, the Thirteenth Amendment ended slavery, completely overturning the parts of the original Constitution that had allowed it. Similarly, Article I of the Constitution originally said that Senators were chosen by state legislatures, but the Seventeenth Amendment overruled that, giving power directly to the people instead, and allowing voters to elect their Senators.

Amendments like these prove that the Constitution isn't set in stone—it's a living document that can be changed when necessary. Each one was created to fix a problem, clarify a rule, or expand rights as America evolved.

Let's break them down one by one! Since each of these amendments was added at different times—and some modify or override previous rules—you'll find the dates and modifications listed under each amendment title. This way, you can see when they were passed, when they became law, and how they changed the Constitution over centuries.

AMENDMENT XI

Limits on Lawsuits Against States

Passed by Congress: March 4, 1794
Ratified: February 7, 1795
Modifies: Part of Article III, Section 2

Can I sue a state in federal court?

"The Judicial power of the United States shall not be construed to extend to any suit in law or equity, commenced or prosecuted against one of the United States by Citizens of another State, or by Citizens or Subjects of any Foreign State."

The Eleventh Amendment says states cannot be sued in federal court by people from other states or other countries. Before this amendment, a citizen from one state could take another state to federal court, which some thought gave the federal government too much power over state matters that should be decided by the states themselves.

For example, today, if you live in Florida and want to sue the state of Georgia in federal court, the Eleventh Amendment blocks that unless Georgia agrees to the lawsuit. However, Americans can still sue their *own* state in state court. There are also some exceptions where lawsuits against states are allowed, such as when a state violates federal laws or constitutional rights.

AMENDMENT XII

Changing Presidential Elections

Passed by Congress: December 9, 1803
Ratified: June 15, 1804
Modifies: Article II, Section 1
Later Modified By: Amendment XX

How did this amendment change Presidential elections?

"The Electors shall meet in their respective states and vote by ballot for President and Vice-President, one of whom, at least, shall not be an inhabitant of the same state with themselves; they shall name in their ballots the person voted for as President, and in distinct ballots the person voted for as Vice-President, and they shall make distinct lists of all persons voted for as President, and of all persons voted for as Vice-President, and of the number of votes for each, which lists they shall sign and certify, and transmit sealed to the seat of the government of the United States, directed to the President of the Senate; — the President of the Senate shall, in the presence of the Senate and House of Representatives, open all the certificates and the votes shall then be counted; — The person having the greatest number of votes for President, shall be the President, if such number be a majority of the whole number of Electors appointed; and if no person have such majority, then from the persons having the highest numbers not exceeding three on the list of those voted for as President, the House of Representatives shall choose immediately, by ballot, the President.

But in choosing the President, the votes shall be taken by states, the representation from each state having one vote; a quorum for this purpose shall consist of a member or members from two-thirds of the states, and a majority of all the states shall be necessary to a choice. And if the House of Representatives shall not choose a President whenever the right of choice shall devolve upon them, before the fourth day of March next following, then the Vice-President shall act as President, as in case of the death or other constitutional disability of the President. — The person having the greatest number of votes as Vice-President, shall be the Vice-President, if such number be a majority of the whole number of Electors appointed, and if no person have a majority, then from the two highest numbers on the list, the Senate shall choose the Vice-President; a quorum for the purpose shall consist of two-thirds of the whole number of Senators, and a majority of the whole number shall be necessary to a choice. But no person constitutionally ineligible to the office of President shall be eligible to that of Vice-President of the United States."

Before the Twelfth Amendment, the Constitution had a different system for electing the President and Vice President. Instead of running as a team, each elector cast two votes for President, with no distinction between first and second choice. The person with the most votes became President, while the runner-up became Vice President. (Remember that from Article II, Section 1?)

At first, this system seemed like a good idea because it was meant to make sure the two best candidates led the country. But once political parties formed in the U.S., it started causing big problems. (Just imagine the difficulties we'd have today if the President and Vice President were from opposing political parties!)

In the Election of 1800, Thomas Jefferson and Aaron Burr were running as a team from the Democratic-Republican Party—Jefferson for President, Burr for Vice President. But since electors had to vote for two people without saying who should have which job, they all voted for both Jefferson and Burr, creating a tie. The Constitution didn't have a backup plan for this, so the House of Representatives had to step in and pick the winner. The decision took days and led to political chaos before Jefferson was finally chosen as President. This exposed a huge flaw in the system: if electors voted for their party's candidates, ties could easily happen again.

The Twelfth Amendment changed the process so that electors now cast one vote for President and a separate vote for Vice President. This way, the person running for Vice President can't accidentally tie with the person running for President. Without this change, the U.S. could still have Presidents and Vice Presidents from opposing parties, making it much harder for the government to function smoothly.

AMENDMENT XIII

Abolishing Slavery

Passed by Congress: January 31, 1865
Ratified: December 6, 1865
Overrides: Article IV, Section 2 (Fugitive Slave Clause)
Makes obsolete: Article I, Section 2 (Three-Fifths Compromise)

The Thirteenth Amendment abolished slavery in the United States, making it illegal everywhere in the country.

> *"Neither slavery nor involuntary servitude, except as a punishment for crime whereof the party shall have been duly convicted, shall exist within the United States, or any place subject to their jurisdiction."*

This was a major turning point in history that changed the country forever. Until this time, slavery was legal in many states, and enslaved people were treated as property, not as citizens with rights.

Why wasn't slavery banned in the original Constitution?

You've already read how the original Constitution allowed slavery to continue. Even though some framers wanted to end it, they compromised to keep the Southern states in the Union and ensure the Constitution was ratified.

At the time, the Southern economy relied on slavery, and many leaders believed that banning it would cause the new country to fall apart before it even began.

Over time, the fight against slavery grew stronger, leading to the Civil War (1861–1865) between the Northern and Southern states. During the war, President Abraham Lincoln issued the Emancipation Proclamation (1863), which freed enslaved people in the Confederate (Southern) states. But that wasn't enough—slavery was still technically legal in some places. The Thirteenth Amendment permanently ended slavery everywhere in the U.S.

What does "involuntary servitude" mean?

This Amendment also banned forced labor ("involuntary servitude"), except as punishment for a crime. That means people can't be forced to work against their will, unless they are serving a prison sentence after being convicted of a crime. Today, some people debate this exception, arguing that it allows unfair work conditions for imprisoned people.

Did this create true equality among all Americans?

Unfortunately, no. This amendment was a huge step forward for civil rights in the U.S., but it didn't automatically mean freedom was equal for everyone. After slavery ended, many states passed racist laws (like Black Codes and later Jim Crow laws) that kept Black Americans from having equal rights. It took more Constitutional amendments, court cases, and civil rights movements to keep fighting for true equality.

AMENDMENT XIV

Citizenship, Equal Protection, and Due Process

Passed by Congress: June 13, 1866
Ratified: July 9, 1868
Overrides: Article I, Section 2 (Three-Fifths Compromise)

The Fourteenth Amendment is one of the most important amendments in U.S. history. It expanded civil rights and protections, defining who is a citizen, guaranteeing equal protection under the law, and ensuring that states follow fair legal procedures.

Originally passed after the Civil War to give freed Black Americans full citizenship and rights, it has since been used to protect everyone's rights in cases involving equality, discrimination, and personal freedoms.

This amendment has played a major role in Supreme Court cases about racial segregation, women's rights, LGBTQ+ rights, and immigrant rights.

The Fourteenth Amendment is the reason that laws must treat people equally and that the U.S. government can't just take away people's rights.

Who is a U.S. citizen?

> *"All persons born or naturalized in the United States, and subject to the jurisdiction thereof, are citizens of the United States and of the State wherein they reside."*

This clause clearly states that if you were born in the U.S., you are automatically a U.S. citizen. This is called birthright citizenship.

Before this amendment, the Constitution didn't clearly define who was a citizen. What's more, in 1857, the Supreme Court ruled in *Dred Scott v. Sandford* that Black Americans could never be citizens, even if they were born in the U.S. The Fourteenth Amendment overturned that court decision, guaranteeing that *anyone* born in the U.S. (or who is a "naturalized" citizen) is fully recognized as a citizen. (Naturalization is the legal process for someone born in another country to become a U.S. citizen.) This part of the amendment is why children born in the U.S. today are automatically U.S. citizens, even if their parents are not.

Can states treat some people differently than others?

> *"No State shall make or enforce any law which shall abridge the privileges or immunities of citizens of the United States; nor shall any State deprive any person of life, liberty, or property, without due process of law; nor deny to any person within its jurisdiction the equal protection of the laws."*

No! The Fourteenth Amendment requires that states treat all citizens fairly and equally under the law. This is called the Equal Protection Clause, and it has been used in many major Supreme Court cases to fight against discrimination. For example, this clause was used in *Brown v. Board of Education* (1954) to end racial segregation in schools. It has also been used in cases involving women's rights, LGBTQ+ rights, and voting rights.

This same section includes the Due Process Clause, which means states can't take away a person's rights or freedoms without fair legal procedures. This protects everyone from unfair punishment or government abuse.

What happens if a state denies people the right to vote?

> *"Representatives shall be apportioned among the several States according to their respective numbers, counting the whole number of persons in each State, excluding Indians not taxed. But when the right to vote at any election for the choice of electors for President and Vice-President of the United States, Representatives in Congress, the Executive and Judicial officers of a State, or the members of the Legislature thereof, is denied to any of the male inhabitants of such State, being twenty-one years of age, and citizens of the United States, or in any way abridged, except for participation in rebellion, or other crime, the basis of representation therein shall be reduced in the proportion which the number of such male citizens shall bear to the whole number of male citizens twenty-one years of age in such State."*

If a state denies people the right to vote, the Fourteenth Amendment says it is supposed to lose some of its representation in the House of Representatives. This section was meant to punish states that restricted voting rights by reducing the number of representatives they get in Congress. The amount of seats lost would be proportional to the number of eligible voters denied the right to vote.

However, this rule was rarely enforced, and Southern states still found ways to limit Black Americans' right to vote through literacy tests (forcing voters to pass unfair reading exams), poll taxes (charging money to vote), and voter intimidation (threatening people to stop them from voting). It wasn't until the Voting Rights Act of 1965 that these tactics were finally banned.

Originally, this section only protected voting rights for men aged 21 and older ("the male inhabitants of such State, being twenty-one years of age"). However, later amendments expanded voting rights beyond this group. The Fifteenth Amendment ensured that states could not deny voting rights based on race, granting Black men the right to vote. The Nineteenth Amendment extended voting rights to women (including Black women), and the Twenty-Sixth Amendment lowered the voting age from 21 to 18. In other words, while the original rule only applied to a certain group, later amendments modified it so that today it includes all American citizens over age 18.

Could former Confederate leaders hold office?

> *"No person shall be a Senator or Representative in Congress, or elector of President and Vice-President, or hold any office, civil or military, under the United States, or under any State, who, having previously taken an oath, as a member of Congress, or as an officer of the United States, or as a member of any State legislature, or as an executive or judicial officer of any State, to support the Constitution of the United States, shall have engaged in insurrection or rebellion against the same, or given aid or comfort to the enemies thereof. But Congress may by a vote of two-thirds of each House, remove such disability."*

After the Civil War, Congress didn't want former Confederate leaders (who had fought against the U.S.) to hold government positions again. They banned people who supported the Confederacy from serving in government roles. However, this wasn't permanent. Congress later passed laws that allowed many of these people to return to politics after they swore loyalty to the U.S.

Did states have to pay debts from the Civil War?

> *"The validity of the public debt of the United States, authorized by law, including debts incurred for payment of pensions and bounties for services in suppressing insurrection or rebellion, shall not be questioned."*

Yes, but only the debts of the Union—the Northern states that fought to keep the U.S. together. This section made it clear that the U.S. government would honor its debts from the Civil War, including paying Union soldiers and others who supported the North during the war.

> *"But neither the United States nor any State shall assume or pay any debt or obligation incurred in aid of insurrection or rebellion against the United States, or any claim for the loss or emancipation of any slave; but all such debts, obligations, and claims shall be held illegal and void."*

However, Confederate states—the Southern states that fought against the U.S. in the Civil War—were responsible for their own war debts. The U.S. government refused to pay for money borrowed by the Confederacy to fund their rebellion, and it also refused to pay former enslavers for losing their enslaved workers after slavery was abolished.

AMENDMENT XV

The Right to Vote Regardless of Race

Passed by Congress: February 26, 1869
Ratified: February 3, 1870
Overrides: State laws that denied voting rights based on race

> "The right of citizens of the United States to vote shall not be denied or abridged by the United States or by any State on account of race, color, or previous condition of servitude."

Did this finally give everyone the right to vote?

No. The Fifteenth Amendment specifically says that voting rights cannot be denied because of "race, color, or previous condition of servitude" (past enslavement). However, it doesn't guarantee the right to vote for everyone.

Before this amendment, many states only allowed white men to vote. The Fifteenth Amendment gave Black men the legal right to vote for the first time. However, it did not apply to women, who had to keep fighting for voting rights until the Nineteenth Amendment was passed more than 50 years later, in 1920.

As we saw in the Fourteenth Amendment, states found ways to work around voting rights protections. Even after the Fifteenth Amendment was ratified, many Southern states still used loopholes like literacy tests, poll taxes, and voter intimidation to block Black Americans from voting. These tactics kept many Black Americans from voting for nearly a century until the Voting Rights Act of 1965 finally put real enforcement behind voting rights protections.

Can states still make their own voting laws?

Yes, but because of the Fifteenth Amendment, states can't use race as a reason to deny voting rights. For example, in the 1960s, the federal government banned literacy tests and poll taxes, which had been used to prevent Black Americans from voting. Today, the Fifteenth Amendment is still cited in Supreme Court cases when people challenge voting laws they believe are discriminatory.

Why does the Fifteenth Amendment still matter today?

The Fifteenth Amendment was a huge step toward equality, but it wasn't the end of the fight for voting rights. Even today, there are debates over voter ID laws, voting restrictions, and election rules, which some argue make it harder for certain groups to vote. It serves as a reminder that voting rights have been fought for—and must continue to be protected.

AMENDMENT XVI

The Federal Income Tax

Passed by Congress: July 2, 1909
Ratified: February 3, 1913
Overrides: Article I, Section 9

> "The Congress shall have power to lay and collect taxes on incomes, from whatever source derived, without apportionment among the several States, and without regard to any census or enumeration."

Did the U.S. always have an income tax?

Nope! Believe it or not, federal income tax actually started in the twentieth century.

Before the Sixteenth Amendment, the federal government couldn't tax people's incomes directly. Instead, it mostly raised money through tariffs (taxes on imported goods) and other indirect taxes.

In 1895, the Supreme Court ruled in *Pollock v. Farmers' Loan & Trust Co.* that a federal income tax was unconstitutional because it violated Article I, Section 9 (which said that direct taxes had to be divided among the states based on population). This made it impossible for the government to tax individuals fairly.

The Sixteenth Amendment changed that, giving Congress the power to collect income taxes from individuals and businesses without dividing the tax among the states.

Why was the Sixteenth Amendment passed?

By the early 1900s, the U.S. government needed more money to fund public services, infrastructure, and national defense. Many people also felt that wealthy individuals and big businesses weren't paying their fair share under the existing tax system. The Sixteenth Amendment allowed Congress to tax people based on how much money they made, ensuring that the government had a steady source of funding. Today, income taxes are the largest source of revenue for the federal government.

Why does the Sixteenth Amendment matter today?

When you get your first job, you will notice money being taken out of your paycheck for taxes. That's because of the Sixteenth Amendment. Without it, the modern income tax system wouldn't exist. The government relies on income taxes to fund essential services like schools, roads, healthcare programs, and national defense.

The amendment also led to the creation of the Internal Revenue Service (IRS) to manage and enforce tax laws. Even today, debates continue over tax rates—who should pay more or less, and how tax money should be spent—but the Sixteenth Amendment permanently gave the federal government the power to tax incomes.

AMENDMENT XVII

Direct Election of Senators

Passed by Congress: May 13, 1912
Ratified: April 8, 1913
Overrides: Article I, Section 3

The Seventeenth Amendment put more power in the hands of the people and helped reduce corruption by making sure Senators answer directly to voters instead of state politicians.

How were Senators originally chosen?

> *"The Senate of the United States shall be composed of two Senators from each State, elected by the people thereof, for six years; and each Senator shall have one vote. The electors in each State shall have the qualifications requisite for electors of the most numerous branch of the State legislatures."*

Before the Seventeenth Amendment, ordinary voters didn't get to choose their U.S. Senators—state legislatures picked them instead. You might remember from Article I, Section 3 that the framers designed it this way so the Senate would be more stable and less influenced by public opinion. The idea was that state governments could make a calmer, less biased choice than the ordinary voters.

But over time, this system led to corruption. Wealthy business leaders sometimes bribed state lawmakers to pick certain Senators, and when politicians in state legislatures couldn't agree, Senate seats sometimes stayed empty for months—or even years.

The Seventeenth Amendment fixed this by letting voters from each state elect their Senators directly—just like they do for members of the House of Representatives. This is still how we elect Senators today.

What if a Senator leaves office during their term?

> *"When vacancies happen in the representation of any State in the Senate, the executive authority of such State shall issue writs of election to fill such vacancies: Provided, That the legislature of any State may empower the executive thereof to make temporary appointments until the people fill the vacancies by election as the legislature may direct."*

Sometimes a Senator leaves office before their term is over, whether due to resignation, expulsion, death, or accepting another position. When this happens, the governor of that state has to call a special election so the voters can choose a new Senator. But instead of leaving the seat empty in the meantime, state legislatures can allow the governor to temporarily appoint a replacement until the election happens. This makes sure that every state always has full representation in the Senate, even if a Senator resigns, passes away, or leaves office for another reason.

Did this change elections for Senators already in office?

> *"This amendment shall not be so construed as to affect the election or term of any Senator chosen before it becomes valid as part of the Constitution."*

No. The Seventeenth Amendment only applied to new elections moving forward. Any Senators who were already elected by state legislatures before the amendment was ratified kept their seats until their terms ended.

AMENDMENT XVIII

Prohibition: The Ban on Alcohol

Passed by Congress: December 18, 1917
Ratified: January 16, 1919
Later Repealed By: Amendment XXI

The Eighteenth Amendment was the first and only amendment to completely ban a product nationwide—alcohol. It is also a rare example of an amendment that was completely overturned later.

Why did the government want to ban alcohol?

In the early 1900s, many people believed alcohol was ruining lives. It was blamed for crime, poverty, domestic violence, and health problems. The Eighteenth Amendment was supposed to solve these problems by banning the making, selling, and transportation of alcohol in the U.S.—a period known as Prohibition.

The government also wanted to crack down on crime linked to alcohol, since saloons and bars were often hotspots for corruption and illegal activity.

But things didn't go as planned. For 13 years, Prohibition led to more crime instead of less. Illegal speakeasies (hidden bars that secretly sold alcohol) popped up everywhere, and bootlegging (smuggling alcohol) became a huge underground business. Organized crime skyrocketed, with powerful gangsters like Al Capone making millions from illegal alcohol sales.

By 1933, it was clear that banning alcohol wasn't working, so the government ended up repealing the Eighteenth Amendment, admitting that Prohibition didn't fix society's problems—it just created new ones.

Did the Eighteenth Amendment ban drinking alcohol?

> *"After one year from the ratification of this article the manufacture, sale, or transportation of intoxicating liquors within, the importation thereof into, or the exportation thereof from the United States and all territory subject to the jurisdiction thereof for beverage purposes is hereby prohibited."*

Not exactly. The Eighteenth Amendment made it illegal to make, sell, or transport alcohol, but it didn't ban *drinking* it. If someone already had alcohol at home, they could technically still drink it, but getting more was a problem since it wasn't legal to buy or sell anymore.

The phrase "after one year from the ratification" meant that the ban wouldn't start immediately—it gave people one year to adjust before Prohibition officially began. This was meant to give businesses time to shut down alcohol production and sales rather than stopping everything overnight.

How did the government enforce this?

> *"The Congress and the several States shall have concurrent power to enforce this article by appropriate legislation."*

This gave both Congress and the states the power to enforce Prohibition. Congress passed the Volstead Act, making it illegal to produce, sell, or transport alcohol, except for medical and religious purposes. The government hired Prohibition agents to shut down illegal breweries and speakeasies, but they couldn't keep up. Alcohol went underground, and bootleggers and gangsters took over the industry, fueling organized crime and corruption.

Did the states want Prohibition, too?

> *"This article shall be inoperative unless it shall have been ratified as an amendment to the Constitution by the legislatures of the several States, as provided in the Constitution, within seven years from the date of the submission hereof to the States by the Congress."*

The Eighteenth Amendment included a rare seven-year time limit, meaning that if enough states didn't approve it within that time, it wouldn't have become law. This was the first amendment to include a deadline for ratification, a practice that later became more common. But Prohibition had strong support at the time, and enough states ratified it before the deadline, making it law in 1919.

AMENDMENT XIX

The Right to Vote for Women

Passed by Congress: June 4, 1919
Ratified: August 18, 1920
Overrides: State laws that denied women the right to vote

For most of U.S. history, voting wasn't a right for all Americans—it was a privilege denied to the majority of people based on race and sex. Just as the Fifteenth Amendment expanded voting rights to Black men (though many were still blocked by racist state laws), the Nineteenth Amendment changed the law for women, giving half of all Americans a right they never had.

This was a huge victory for women and civil rights, but it wasn't just handed over. Women fought for decades, facing arrests, public shaming, and even violence just for demanding the right to vote. They organized protests, endured hunger strikes, and challenged politicians who insisted that women didn't belong in the voting booth, refusing to back down until change became inevitable.

With this in mind, let's read the short but powerful text of this amendment and then break down its significance:

> "The right of citizens of the United States to vote shall not be denied or abridged by the United States or by any State on account of sex.
>
> "Congress shall have power to enforce this article by appropriate legislation."

Wait, women seriously didn't get the right to vote until a little over 100 years ago?

That's right. For nearly 150 years of U.S. history, the voices of women were missing at the ballot box.

When the Constitution was written, voting rights were left up to the states, and nearly all of them only allowed men to vote. By the late 1800s, some Western states began granting women the right to vote in state and local elections, but in most of the country, women had no voting rights at any level. Even in states where women could vote locally, they were still barred from federal elections, meaning they had no say in choosing the President, Senators, or Representatives.

The Nineteenth Amendment finally forced every state to recognize women's voting rights, making sure that no woman—no matter where she lived—was denied a say in her own government.

Did all women, regardless of race, get the right to vote?

Yes and no. The Nineteenth Amendment guaranteed women the right to vote, but many states still found ways to prevent women of color from voting. They passed racist laws that used loopholes to make voting harder for Black, Native American, Asian, and Latina women.

These were the same tactics used to suppress Black men's votes, including literacy tests (forcing voters to pass unfair reading exams), poll taxes (charging money to vote, which many couldn't afford), and voter intimidation (threatening or harassing people to keep them from voting).

Because of these barriers, many women of color weren't fully able to exercise their right to vote until the Voting Rights Act of 1965, which finally outlawed these discriminatory practices.

How did women win the right to vote?

For decades, women fought for their right to vote in a movement called women's suffrage (suffrage means "the right to vote"). Activists like Susan B. Anthony, Elizabeth Cady Stanton, Sojourner Truth, Ida B. Wells, and Alice Paul led protests, marches, and hunger strikes to demand voting rights. Many women were arrested and jailed for simply speaking out, including Susan B. Anthony, who was fined for voting illegally in 1872.

After years of pressure, Congress finally passed the Nineteenth Amendment in 1919, and enough states ratified it by 1920, making it law.

Now that all women have the right to vote, does this amendment still matter?

Absolutely. The Nineteenth Amendment was a huge victory, but it was just one step in a longer fight for equal rights. When voting rights expand, it doesn't just help one group—it paves the way for others. The fight for women's suffrage inspired later movements that led to:

- The Voting Rights Act of 1965 (protecting Black voters)
- The Twenty-Sixth Amendment of 1971 (lowering the voting age to 18)
- The Americans with Disabilities Act of 1990 (making voting more accessible)

Women's involvement in elections has skyrocketed since the ratification of the Nineteenth Amendment. In fact, in every U.S. presidential election since 1980, women have turned out to vote at higher rates than men!

Was the U.S. a leader in women's voting rights?

Believe it or not, as "overdue" as this amendment was, many major countries still hadn't granted women voting rights—and wouldn't for decades. When the U.S. finally ratified the Nineteenth Amendment in 1920, women still couldn't vote in France until 1944, Japan until 1945, Mexico until 1953, Switzerland not until 1971, and Saudi Arabia only granted women the right to vote in 2015.

So while the U.S. took too long, it was still ahead of many nations in the global push for women's suffrage. The British suffrage movement was active at the same time, but women in the United Kingdom only won partial voting rights in 1918, with full suffrage in 1928—eight years after the U.S.

American suffragists also played a role in shaping the fight for women's voting rights worldwide. The National American Woman Suffrage Association (NAWSA) co-founded the International Woman Suffrage Alliance in 1904. This global network connected suffragists across Europe, Canada, and beyond, spreading strategies and inspiration to movements in other countries.

While the U.S. wasn't the first—New Zealand led the way in 1893—American activists helped fuel the broader fight for equality, showing that the struggle for women's political power was a global movement.

AMENDMENT XX

The Lame Duck Amendment

Passed by Congress: March 2, 1932
Ratified: January 23, 1933
Modifies: Article I, Section 4 and Article II, Section 1

For most of U.S. history, newly elected Presidents and Congress members had to wait months before officially taking office. This delay—called the "lame duck" period—meant that outgoing officials who had lost the election still had power for a long time, sometimes making decisions that didn't reflect the will of the voters.

The Twentieth Amendment made sure new leaders will take office quickly instead of letting defeated officials hold onto power for months. It also clarified the process for handling Presidential transitions and unexpected situations, making sure the government keeps running smoothly no matter what happens after an election.

When does a new President take office?

> *"The terms of the President and the Vice President shall end at noon on the 20th day of January, and the terms of Senators and Representatives at noon on the 3d day of January, of the years in which such terms would have ended if this article had not been ratified; and the terms of their successors shall then begin."*

The Twentieth Amendment moved up the dates when Presidents, Vice Presidents, and Congress members take office. This shortened the lame duck period, making sure the government transitions faster after elections.

Before this amendment, Presidents were elected in November but didn't take office until March. This long wait made sense in the 1700s, when travel and communication were slow, but by the 1930s, it was outdated.

The Twentieth Amendment moved Inauguration Day to January 20. This means that when a new President is elected in November, they take office just two months later instead of four.

When does the new Congress start working?

> *"The Congress shall assemble at least once in every year, and such meeting shall begin at noon on the 3d day of January, unless they shall by law appoint a different day."*

Just like the Presidency, Congress also had a long delay before starting work. Previously, a new Congress didn't officially begin until March, meaning the old Congress stayed in power for months after an election. The Twentieth Amendment moved the start date for Congress to January 3, making sure newly-elected lawmakers can get to work faster after an election. (And if you're wondering, "3d" isn't a typo—that's how they wrote "3rd"!)

What if a President-elect dies before taking office?

> *"If, at the time fixed for the beginning of the term of the President, the President elect shall have died, the Vice President elect shall become President."*

This part of the amendment clarifies what would happen if a newly-elected President dies before taking office. Before, the Constitution didn't say what to do in this situation. This clause clarifies that if a President-elect dies before Inauguration Day, the Vice President-elect automatically becomes President.

What happens if we can't choose a President in time?

> "If a President shall not have been chosen before the time fixed for the beginning of his term, or if the President elect shall have failed to qualify, then the Vice President elect shall act as President until a President shall have qualified..."

This means that if there is a problem with the election—for example, if no candidate wins a majority of electoral votes—the Vice President-elect takes over as acting President until a winner is determined.

What happens if we can't choose a President in time?

> "and the Congress may by law provide for the case wherein neither a President elect nor a Vice President elect shall have qualified, declaring who shall then act as President, or the manner in which one who is to act shall be selected, and such person shall act accordingly until a President or Vice President shall have qualified."

This means that if there is no President-elect and no Vice President-elect (for example, if an election is delayed or disputed), Congress can pass a law deciding who should act as President until someone qualifies. Congress later used this power to pass the Presidential Succession Act, which explains the order of who takes over if the President and Vice President can't serve (for example, the Speaker of the House is next in line after the Vice President).

What if a candidate dies while they're deciding the winner?

> *"The Congress may by law provide for the case of the death of any of the persons from whom the House of Representatives may choose a President whenever the right of choice shall have devolved upon them, and for the case of the death of any of the persons from whom the Senate may choose a Vice President whenever the right of choice shall have devolved upon them."*

If no candidate wins a majority of electoral votes, the House of Representatives chooses the President, and the Senate chooses the Vice President (as outlined in the Twelfth Amendment).

Did this amendment take effect immediately?

> *"Sections 1 and 2 shall take effect on the 15th day of October following the ratification of this article.*
>
> *"This article shall be inoperative unless it shall have been ratified as an amendment to the Constitution by the legislatures of three-fourths of the several States within seven years from the date of its submission."*

Even though the amendment was ratified on January 23, 1933, the new start dates for Presidents and Congress didn't go into effect until October of that year. And just like the Eighteenth Amendment (Prohibition) and some later amendments, the Twentieth Amendment had a seven-year deadline for ratification. If not enough states had approved it within that time, it wouldn't have become law.

AMENDMENT XXI

The End of Prohibition

Passed by Congress: February 20, 1933
Ratified: December 5, 1933
Modifies: The Eighteenth Amendment

You will remember that the Eighteenth Amendment banned alcohol across the U.S. to reduce crime and improve society. But instead of solving problems, Prohibition fueled organized crime, corruption, and illegal drinking.

After thirteen years, the government admitted it wasn't working. The Twenty-First Amendment repealed the Eighteenth Amendment, making alcohol legal again and returning control over alcohol laws to individual states. This is the only amendment in U.S. history that completely overturned another amendment. It also set a precedent for how states control alcohol laws, which is why different states still have different rules today.

Did Prohibition end immediately?

> *"The eighteenth article of amendment to the Constitution of the United States is hereby repealed."*

Yes! This amendment completely erased the Eighteenth Amendment, which had banned alcohol in the U.S. since 1920. However, while alcohol became legal again, that didn't mean it was suddenly available everywhere. States still had the power to regulate alcohol—and some states continued banning it for years after Prohibition officially ended.

Who decides alcohol laws now?

> *"The transportation or importation into any State, Territory, or possession of the United States for delivery or use therein of intoxicating liquors, in violation of the laws thereof, is hereby prohibited."*

The Twenty-First Amendment gave states total control over alcohol laws. This meant that:

- States could decide their own drinking ages (until the federal government later set it to 21 in 1984).
- Some counties and towns could choose to stay "dry" (meaning alcohol was still illegal there).
- States could regulate how alcohol is sold, taxed, and distributed.

Even today, alcohol laws vary widely by state—some have strict sales limits, some allow alcohol delivery, and others still have dry counties where selling alcohol is banned.

Did the public have a say in repealing Prohibition?

> *"This article shall be inoperative unless it shall have been ratified as an amendment to the Constitution by conventions in the several States, as provided in the Constitution, within seven years from the date of the submission hereof to the States by the Congress."*

Prohibition failed so badly that Congress didn't just want to repeal it—they wanted to make sure the process was fast and fair. Instead of having state legislatures vote on it, they used state conventions, where elected delegates directly voted on the amendment. This method made sure that lawmakers couldn't block the repeal if the voters wanted it gone. It worked—the amendment was ratified in less than a year, making it one of the fastest amendments ever passed.

AMENDMENT XXII

Presidential Term Limits

Passed by Congress: March 21, 1947
Ratified: February 27, 1951
Modifies: The original Constitution,
which did not set a term limit

The Twenty-Second Amendment set a two-term limit on the Presidency, making sure no one could serve for more than eight years (except in special cases).

How long can a President be in office?

> *"No person shall be elected to the office of the President more than twice, and no person who has held the office of President, or acted as President, for more than two years of a term to which some other person was elected President shall be elected to the office of the President more than once."*

This means:

- A President can only be elected twice—two four-year terms—for a total of eight years).
- If a Vice President or another official steps in as President for more than two years of someone else's term, they can only be elected once afterward. So, in a rare case where a Vice President takes over for a President who leaves office early, they might serve up to 10 years—two years finishing the previous President's term, plus two full terms of their own.

Before this amendment, there was no official rule about how many terms a President could serve. Most Presidents followed the example set by George Washington, who voluntarily stepped down after two terms, believing that no one should hold power for too long.

But then came Franklin D. Roosevelt (FDR), who was elected four times. He as President from 1933 to 1945, and died just a few months into his fourth term, serving a little over 12 years. His long time in office made people worried about one person holding too much power for too long.

Was this rule aimed at the President at the time?

> *"But this Article shall not apply to any person holding the office of President when this Article was proposed by the Congress, and shall not prevent any person who may be holding the office of President, or acting as President, during the term within which this Article becomes operative from holding the office of President or acting as President during the remainder of such term."*

No. When the Twenty-Second Amendment was passed, Harry Truman was President, and this rule specifically makes sure it didn't apply to him. In fact, since he was in his second term in office when the amendment was proposed, he could have run for a third term—but he chose not to.

So was this amendment aimed at FDR?

Yes and no. When FDR was elected to a third and fourth term, the U.S. was in crisis. The Great Depression and World War II made a lot of Americans believe that switching

Presidents mid-crisis would be too risky. So, they kept re-electing him. But after he died in 1945, people started reconsidering whether one person should stay in power for that long.

Congress moved quickly to make the two-term tradition an official rule, so that no future President stay in office forever. Today, the two-term limit remains in place, ensuring that the U.S. President can serve a maximum of eight years.

Did this amendment have a time limit for ratification?

> *"This article shall be inoperative unless it shall have been ratified as an amendment to the Constitution by the legislatures of three-fourths of the several States within seven years from the date of its submission to the States by the Congress."*

Yes! Like several other amendments, the Twenty-Second Amendment had a seven-year deadline for states to ratify it. If enough states hadn't approved it in time, it wouldn't have become law.

AMENDMENT XXIII

Giving Washington, D.C. Electoral Votes

Passed by Congress: June 16, 1960
Ratified: March 29, 1961
Modifies: The original Constitution, which did not give Washington, D.C. representation in presidential elections

This amendment finally gave the people of Washington, D.C. a voice in presidential elections, but it also highlighted the issue of D.C.'s lack of full representation.

> "The District constituting the seat of Government of the United States shall appoint in such manner as the Congress may direct:
>
> A number of electors of President and Vice President equal to the whole number of Senators and Representatives in Congress to which the District would be entitled if it were a State, but in no event more than the least populous State; they shall be in addition to those appointed by the States, but they shall be considered, for the purposes of the election of President and Vice President, to be electors appointed by a State; and they shall meet in the District and perform such duties as provided by the twelfth article of amendment."

What does the amendment actually change?

This made it law that:

- Washington, D.C. gets electoral votes in presidential elections, just like a state.
- The number of electoral votes D.C. gets can't be higher than the smallest state's number of electors.

How many electoral votes does Washington, D.C. have?

This amendment limits D.C.'s electoral votes at the same number as the least populated state. Since the smallest states have three electoral votes (two Senators and at least one Representative), D.C. was given three electoral votes as well. Even though today D.C. has more people than some states, it can never have more than three electors, no matter how much its population grows.

Could people in Washington, D.C. vote for President before this?

No. Believe it or not, before this amendment, residents of Washington, D.C. had zero say in presidential elections. Since D.C. is not a state, it wasn't included in the Electoral College system set up in the Constitution. That meant that even though over 700,000 U.S. citizens lived in D.C. by 1960, they couldn't vote for President—even though the federal government was based in their city!

Did this amendment give D.C. full representation in the federal government?

No. While the Twenty-Third Amendment let D.C. residents vote for President, it did not give them full representation in Congress.

Even today:

- D.C. has no Senators at all. Unlike states, which each have two U.S. Senators, D.C. has zero representation in the Senate.
- D.C. has one delegate in the House of Representatives—but they cannot vote on final laws. They can introduce bills, serve on committees, and debate legislation, but they do not have a final vote on passing laws.

Because of this, many people argue that D.C. residents are still being denied equal representation in their own government. They pay federal taxes, serve in the military, and follow the same laws as every other U.S. citizen—yet they have no voting power in Congress. This has fueled a growing movement to make D.C. a state, with many activists and lawmakers fighting to give D.C. full representation, just like every other state.

AMENDMENT XXIV

Banning the Poll Tax

Passed by Congress: August 27, 1962
Ratified: January 23, 1964
Overrides: State laws that required poll taxes as a condition for voting

The Twenty-Fourth Amendment finally banned poll taxes in federal elections, making sure that no one could be charged money just to exercise their right to vote.

> "The right of citizens of the United States to vote in any primary or other election for President or Vice President, for electors for President or Vice President, or for Senator or Representative in Congress, shall not be denied or abridged by the United States or any State by reason of failure to pay any poll tax or other tax."

What is a poll tax, and why was it banned?

A poll tax was a fee that people were required to pay in order to vote. Southern states often used these taxes as a tactic to keep Black Americans, women, and poor citizens from voting, despite their constitutional right to do so.

Since many couldn't afford the fee, poll taxes became a deliberate barrier to suppress their votes. They didn't technically break the law but they still blocked access to the ballot box. Even though the tax applied to everyone, it disproportionately hurt marginalized communities, making it nearly impossible for many to participate in democracy.

Can the federal government still make people pay to vote?

No. This amendment clearly states that poll taxes (and any other fee to vote) are illegal in federal elections. But some states still continued using them in state and local elections.

It wasn't until 1966, in the Supreme Court case *Harper v. Virginia Board of Elections*, that poll taxes were ruled unconstitutional at all levels, officially ending them in state and local elections as well.

What about today? Is there still voter suppression?

The Twenty-Fourth Amendment was a huge victory for civil rights and a step toward making elections more fair. But even today, there are still debates about voter suppression, with some states passing laws that make it harder for certain groups to vote—like requiring strict voter ID laws or limiting early voting and mail-in ballots. In other words, the fight for voting rights didn't end with this amendment, which is why efforts to protect fair and equal access to voting continue today.

AMENDMENT XXV

Presidential Succession and Disability

Passed by Congress: July 6, 1965
Ratified: February 10, 1967
Overrides: Parts of Article II, Section 1

For most of U.S. history, the Constitution didn't fully explain what happens if a President can't do their job. The Vice President was supposed to take over if the President died or resigned, but there were big gaps in the rules—what if the President was alive but too sick to lead? What if there was no Vice President to take over? This amendment cleared up these issues by officially laying out the process for replacing a President or Vice President when necessary.

If the President leaves office, who takes over?

> *"In case of the removal of the President from office or of his death or resignation, the Vice President shall become President."*

This part is simple—if the President dies, resigns, or is removed from office (like through impeachment), the Vice President immediately becomes President.

By the time this was pass in 1965, this had already been the tradition (like when Vice President Lyndon B. Johnson became President after John F. Kennedy was assassinated in 1963), but this amendment made it an official part of the Constitution.

What about if there is no Vice President?

> *"Whenever there is a vacancy in the office of the Vice President, the President shall nominate a Vice President who shall take office upon confirmation by a majority vote of both Houses of Congress."*

Before this amendment, if the Vice President left office for any reason—whether they became President, resigned, died, or were removed—there was no way to replace them until the next election. That meant the U.S. sometimes went years without a Vice President, which was risky if something happened to the President.

The Twenty-Fifth Amendment fixed this by allowing the President to nominate a new Vice President if the position becomes vacant—but that person must be approved by Congress. This rule ensures there is always someone next in line for the Presidency, even during times of crisis.

This part of the amendment has been used twice. In 1973, Vice President Spiro Agnew resigned, so President Richard Nixon chose Gerald Ford as his replacement. Less than a year later, Nixon himself resigned, making Ford President. Then, Ford chose Nelson Rockefeller to be his new Vice President.

Who if the President needs to step away temporarily?

> *"Whenever the President transmits to the President pro tempore of the Senate and the Speaker of the House of Representatives his written declaration that he is unable to discharge the powers and duties of his office, and until he transmits to them a*

> written declaration to the contrary, such powers and duties shall be discharged by the Vice President as Acting President."

If the President knows they won't be able to do their job for a short time, they can temporarily transfer power to the Vice President. This is called "voluntary transfer of power." This has happened several times—for example, when Presidents Ronald Reagan and George W. Bush had medical procedures, they briefly gave power to their Vice Presidents until they recovered. Once the President is ready to return, they send a written notice, and power is transferred back to them.

What happens if the President is unable to serve but doesn't (or can't) step down?

> "Whenever the Vice President and a majority of either the principal officers of the executive departments or of such other body as Congress may by law provide, transmit to the President pro tempore of the Senate and the Speaker of the House of Representatives their written declaration that the President is unable to discharge the powers and duties of his office, the Vice President shall immediately assume the powers and duties of the office as Acting President."

This part of the Twenty-Fifth Amendment is much more serious. It allows the Vice President and a majority of the President's Cabinet (the heads of government departments) to declare that the President is unable to serve—even if the President doesn't agree. This is called "involuntary transfer of power."

If the Vice President and Cabinet agree that the President can't serve, the Vice President immediately takes over as Acting President. However, this isn't permanent—the President can try to take back power by sending a letter to Congress saying they are fine. If the Vice President and Cabinet still agree that the President can't serve, Congress votes on whether the President stays removed from office. If two-thirds of both the House and Senate agree, the President is officially removed from power, and the Vice President takes over permanently.

Can the President fight the decision to remove them?

> *"Thereafter, when the President transmits to the President pro tempore of the Senate and the Speaker of the House of Representatives his written declaration that no inability exists, he shall resume the powers and duties of his office unless the Vice President and a majority of either the principal officers of the executive department or of such other body as Congress may by law provide, transmit within four days to the President pro tempore of the Senate and the Speaker of the House of Representatives their written declaration that the President is unable to discharge the powers and duties of his office. Thereupon Congress shall decide the issue, assembling within forty-eight hours for that purpose if not in session. If the Congress, within twenty-one days after receipt of the latter written declaration, or, if Congress is not in session, within twenty-one days after Congress is required to assemble, determines by two-thirds vote of both Houses that the President is unable to discharge the powers and duties of his office, the Vice President*

> *shall continue to discharge the same as Acting President; otherwise, the President shall resume the powers and duties of his office."*

Yes. If the President is removed but believes they are still able to lead, they can send a letter saying they are fit to serve again. However, if the Vice President and the Cabinet *still* think the President is unfit, they can send another declaration to Congress within four days, keeping the President from resuming power. Then, Congress must vote on the issue. If two-thirds of both the House and Senate agree that the President is unable to serve, the Vice President stays in charge. If Congress doesn't reach that two-thirds vote, the President gets their power back.

Has a President ever been removed this way?

No, an "involuntary transfer of power" has never been fully used to permanently remove a President. However, it has been discussed and debated at times when some people believed a President was too sick, unstable, or unable to lead. While it's a safety measure to protect the country, using it would be a huge political decision, and it remains untested in U.S. history.

AMENDMENT XXVI

Lowering the Voting Age to 18

Passed by Congress: March 23, 1971
Ratified: July 1, 1971
Overrides: State laws that set the voting age higher than 18

The Twenty-Sixth Amendment gave millions of young people the right to vote by lowering the voting age from 21 to 18, which was already the legal age of adulthood. This ensured all adults have a say in the government decisions that affected their lives.

What exactly did this amendment do?

> *"The right of citizens of the United States, who are eighteen years of age or older, to vote shall not be denied or abridged by the United States or by any State on account of age."*

Before this amendment, most states set the voting age at 21, even though 18-year-olds were legally considered adults. This meant millions of young people could work, pay taxes, and even be drafted into war—but they couldn't vote.

Why were young people fighting so hard for this right?

The biggest push to lower the voting age came during the Vietnam War. Eighteen-year-olds were being sent to fight and die, yet they had no say in choosing the leaders making those decisions. This sparked protests and a powerful rallying cry: "Old enough to fight, old enough to vote."

After years of protests and activism, Congress passed the Twenty-Sixth Amendment, guaranteeing that any U.S. citizen who is 18 or older has the right to vote, no matter what state they live in.

Could states still set their own voting ages?

> *"The Congress shall have power to enforce this article by appropriate legislation."*

No. Before this amendment, states had the power to set their own voting ages, and most required voters to be at least 21. The Twenty-Sixth Amendment overruled those state laws, making sure that all states allowed 18-year-olds to vote in every election—local, state, and federal.

How did the lower voting age change elections?

The Twenty-Sixth Amendment completely changed elections by adding millions of young voters to the mix.

Lowering the voting age to 18 meant young people could finally have a say in decisions that directly shaped their future—war, education, jobs, and more.

For the first time, university students had real political power. Instead of protesting for the right to vote, they could campaign, organize, and actually elect leaders who could make change happen. Campus activism became stronger because students weren't just fighting to be heard—they were taking action and influencing real policies.

This amendment forced politicians to take young voters seriously. Leaders could no longer ignore the issues young people cared about because their votes now had the power to sway elections.

Young people fought hard for this right. Yet, today, they vote at lower rates than older generations. If reading the Constitution and its many amendments has shown you anything, it's that change is possible. Ideas which once seemed impossible can become law when people demand it.

Your vote is your voice. Don't waste it!

AMENDMENT XXVII

Delaying Congressional Pay Raises

Passed by Congress: September 25, 1789
Ratified: May 7, 1992
Adds: How and when Congress can increase its own salary

This amendment prevents Congress from immediately giving itself a raise without voter approval. And it has a really cool story behind it. Believe it or not, this amendment was originally proposed in 1789—at the same time as the Bill of Rights—but it wasn't ratified until 1992!

Who sets the salary for members of Congress?

> *"No law, varying the compensation for the services of the Senators and Representatives, shall take effect, until an election of Representatives shall have intervened."*

Congress has always been able to set its members' salaries. But this amendment stops them from giving themselves an instant raise.

If Congress decides to increase their pay, the raise won't take effect until after the next election. That way, if voters don't agree with the pay raise, they have a chance to vote those lawmakers out before it takes effect.

While this amendment doesn't stop Congress from raising its own salary, it makes sure they have to answer to the public first—keeping them accountable.

Why did it take over 200 years to pass?

This amendment was proposed alongside the Bill of Rights in 1789, but while the first ten amendments were ratified quickly, this one was ignored for over two centuries. Then, in the 1980s, a college student named Gregory Watson discovered that the amendment had never been officially rejected—it had been passed by Congress and then forgotten. Realizing it could still become law, he launched a one-man campaign to get states to ratify it. Amazingly, his efforts worked. By 1992, enough states had approved it, making it the longest ratification process in U.S. history.

Watson's story is proof that young people aren't just observers of history—they can shape it. If a single determined college student could change the U.S. Constitution, imagine what you could do.

Your Rights, Your Voice, Your Future

You made it. You've read through the Constitution, the Bill of Rights, and every amendment that has shaped the United States into what it is today. That means you now have something powerful: a real, working knowledge of how American law actually functions. You know what your rights are, where they come from, and how they've changed over time. Just as importantly, you understand that the Constitution isn't set in stone—it was designed to grow, adapt, and be challenged.

So, what do you do with that knowledge?

You use it. You question what you hear. You pay attention when politicians, media and community leaders talk about your rights. You stay engaged—whether that means voting, speaking up in conversations, or making sure your friends and family understand their rights, too.

You know that laws aren't perfect, that they were written by people just like you, and that they directly impact your life. You also know that those laws can change—but only when people demand it.

You don't have to run for office or go to law school to make an impact (although if that's your path, we need leaders like you!). Simply knowing the facts, sharing them, and making sure others understand their rights is already a powerful way to create change.

The truth is, the Constitution only works if people understand it. It's not some distant, untouchable document that only politicians and lawyers deal with—it's the foundation of the freedoms you use every single day. And history has shown that young people just like you are often the ones leading the charge for change. The Constitution protects your rights, but it's up to you to make sure they are respected, upheld, and expanded when necessary.

The more you know, the more powerful your voice becomes. Voting isn't just a right—it's a tool, a way to actively shape the laws and policies that affect your daily life. And if you aren't old enough to vote yet, or you aren't a citizen, that doesn't mean you're powerless. Some of the biggest movements in history have been fueled by young people who knew their rights, spoke up, and refused to let others decide their future for them.

The Constitution is yours. The future is yours. What happens next? That's up to you.

Vote!

Voting is your democratic superpower.

This section gives you everything you need to use it. From eligibility rules to key resources, you'll find tools to become an informed, confident voter. Plus, a voting checklist to keep you on track, so when Election Day comes, you're ready to make an impact.

Why Should I Vote?

Voting is one of the most powerful ways to make an impact—but only if you actually use it. You've seen how many people fought for this right, and now it's in your hands. Every election shapes the laws, leaders, and policies that affect your daily life. If you don't vote, someone else is making those decisions for you.

Every Election Counts

Voting isn't just about the presidential race every four years. State and local elections happen all the time. In your state, there's an election at least every two years—sometimes more often! These elections often have a bigger impact on your daily life than national ones, yet they get the lowest turnout. That's a problem.

Why should I care about state and local elections?

State elections are where you vote for your Governor, U.S. Senators, and Representatives. But you also vote for "down-ballot" candidates (officials who control key decisions in your community) including:

- **Mayor:** Runs your city and oversees public services
- **City council members:** Pass local laws that affect housing, public safety, and business regulations
- **State legislators:** Make laws for your entire state on issues including education, wages, and healthcare
- **School board members:** Decide how local schools are funded and what resources they get

These state and local leaders shape the policies that impact your daily life, including:

- **Climate and environmental laws:** Protecting the environment starts at the local level. It's not just federal policy that dictates environmental protections—state and local leaders make key decisions about clean energy, water safety, pollution control, and conservation.
- **School funding:** Electing leaders who prioritize education can mean more money, new textbooks, and improved facilities for your local schools.
- **Reproductive rights:** Whether abortion and other reproductive healthcare is legal in your state is decided by state lawmakers and governors, elected by people like you who show up to vote.
- **Gun laws:** The strength of your state's gun safety laws depends on who's in office. State lawmakers and governors make these decisions, not the federal government.
- **Minimum wage laws:** Do you want to make more than $7.25 an hour? Many states have raised their minimum wage, and others can still choose to increase it. If you want higher wages where you live, state lawmakers—not the President—are the ones who decide.
- **Housing policies:** Your mayor and city council set the rules on rent control, housing assistance, and zoning laws—deciding how affordable and accessible housing is in your area.

These are real issues that impact your daily life. If you don't vote, other people will make those choices for you—and you may not like the results.

Am I Eligible to Vote?

You can vote in the U.S. if:

- **You are a U.S. citizen**
- **You are at least 18 years old**
  Some states let 17-year-olds to vote in primaries if they'll be 18 by Election Day
- **You meet your state's residency requirements**
  Find these listed on vote.gov

Helpful Websites

BallotReady.org – Research candidates, elections, and ballot measures you can vote on, based on your location.

GenerationCitizen.org – Get involved in community action projects and make a difference where you live.

MyReps.DataMade.us – Find all your representatives and how to contact them by entering your address.

PolitiFact.com – Fact-check statements from politicians and the media with this Pulitzer Prize-winning site that helps you separate truth from misinformation.

RockTheVote.org – Join other young Americans to advocate for voting rights and get involved in shaping our democracy through education and activism.

Vote.gov – Find out how to vote if you're a new citizen, have a disability, live overseas, or are a college student, military member, or unhoused voter.

My Voting Checklist

*✓ Do all these things at **nass.org/can-I-vote** and share this list with friends and family!*

- [ ] **Check my voter registration status**
    - [ ] *See if I'm already registered. (Check before every election.)*
    - [ ] *Update it if I moved, changed my name, or just turned 18.*

- [ ] **Register to vote, if needed**
    - [ ] *Find out my state's registration deadline.*
    - [ ] *Register online, in person, or by mail.*

- [ ] **Know my state's voting rules**
    - [ ] *Check if I need an ID to vote.*
    - [ ] *See if I can vote early, by mail, or where my polling place is.*
    - [ ] *Learn if my polling place has wheelchair access, voting aids for blind and deaf voters, or other voter assistance if needed.*

- [ ] **Request a mail-in or absentee ballot**
    - [ ] *If voting by mail, request my mail-in or absentee ballot.*
    - [ ] *Check (and double check) my state's rules and deadlines for mail-in ballots.*

- [ ] **See what's on my ballot**
    - [ ] *Research candidates and measures on the ballot.*
    - [ ] *Learn about my local, state, and national elections.*
    - [ ] *Decide who and what I will vote for before Election Day.*

- [ ] **Make a voting plan**
    - [ ] ***Voting by mail or absentee?***
      Know mail-in deadlines and where to send it or drop it off.
    - [ ] ***Voting in person early?***
      Find out when and where, and bring my ID (if needed).
    - [ ] ***Voting in person on Election Day?***
      Double check my voting location, hours, and date. Plan my ride, timing, and bring my ID (if needed).

- [ ] **VOTE!** ✌
    - [ ] ***In person:*** *Bring a charged phone and be ready for lines. If I'm in line when polls close, I can still vote so stay in line! Having issues? Call Election Protection: 866-OUR-VOTE.*
    - [ ] ***By mail:*** *Send in my ballot by my state's deadline.*

www.ingramcontent.com/pod-product-compliance
Lightning Source LLC
Chambersburg PA
CBHW060318050426
42449CB00011B/2532